MOSCOW

Saint Petersburg
2012

MOSCOW

Text by T. Geidor, P. Pavlinov and A. Raskin

Design by N. Kutovoy

Translated from the Russian by J. Redkina

Photography by
Yu. Artamonov – *ill. 255, 284, 314*
V. Baranovsky – *ill. 172, 195, 276*
R. Beniaminson – *ill. 307*
P. Demidov – *ill. 232*
V. Filippov – *ill. 366, 367*
A. Goriainov – *ill. 193, 280, 283, 296, 352*
Yu. and O. Grigorov – *ill. 418*
V. Khmelevsky – *ill. 354–356, 358, 359*
K. Kokoshkin – ill. *182, 186,194, 198, 207, 285, 291, 308–310, 312,*
319–323, 325, 327, 335, 379, 381, 388, 392, 395, 399–401, 404
V. Korniushin – *ill. 215, 237, 251, 288, 315, 351, 418*
V. Mendeleyev – *ill. 81*
A. Minin – *ill. 406*
A. Petrosian – *cover, ill. 173, 174, 180, 181, 199, 206, 212, 236, 295, 297,*
299–302, 333, 344, 346, 347, 375, 380, 396, 402, p. 304
V. Poliakov – *ill. 2, 9, 15, 183, 210, 222, 250, 326, 328, 334, 343, 350,*
365, 370, 382, 386, 407, 409
N. Rakhmanov – *cover, pp. 1, 4–5, 7–10, 12–13, ill. 1, 4–8, 10–14, 16–80,*
82–108, 110–171, 175, 179, 184, 185, 187–192, 196, 200–205, 208, 209,
211, 213, 214, 216–221, 223–225, 238–249, 252–254, 256, 259, 260, 267,
275, 277, 281, 282, 286, 290, 293, 303, 311, 317, 318, 331, 332, 336–342,
345, 348, 349, 353, 357, 362–364, 368, 369, 371–374,376–378, 379, 383–385,
389–391, 403, 408, 411, 412, 414, 416, 417, 420–425, 427, 429, 431, 432,
pp. 302–303
V. Savik – *ill. 313, 415, 419, 426, 428, 430, 433*
G. Shpikalov – *cover, pp. 2–3, ill. 397, 405*
V. Solomatin – *ill. 360, 361*
E. Steinert – *ill. 109, 324, 329, 330*
O. Trubsky – *ill. 232*
V. Vdovin – *ill. 287, 294*
A. Viktorov – *ill. 258*
V. Vorontsov – *ill. 292*
E. Yezhov – *ill. 197, 393, 394, 398*
A. Zakharchenko – *ill. 304*
RIA Novosti – *ill. 245, 246*

Editors I. Lvova and I. Kharitonowa

Computer layout by S. Bashun

Colour correction by V. Bykovsky, V. Kniazev and A. Miagkov

Moscow... The very word has a majestic and powerful resonance. It almost seems to glow with the same brilliance as the golden domes of the city's churches and the burnished frames of their miraculous icons. The French writer and traveller, Marquis Adolphe de Custine, once noted the city's unique aura. A harsh critic of Russia, which he visited in 1839, Custine was nonetheless inspired by the beauty of Moscow: "The play of light that bathes this ethereal city is a waking phantasmagoria, which makes Moscow one of a kind, without match in Europe." In his novel "War and Peace," Tolstoy describes the radiance that emanated from the ancient capital of Russia as Napoleon viewed it from Poklonny Hill on 2 September 1812: "The brightness of the morning was magical. Moscow seen from Poklonny Hill lay spaciously spread out with her river, her gardens, and her churches, and she seemed to be living her usual life, her cupolas glittering like stars in the sunlight."

Moscow's stellar brilliance is symbolic of its historical role as the gatherer of the Russian lands, the first capital where princes and tsars were crowned in an act that lent legitimacy to the authority of the individual brought to the throne, be they the natural heir or another member of the ruling family. Moscow took root in the very heart of the Russian lands and gradually became immortal. Although it was repeatedly burned to the ground, it rose from the ashes each time like the phoenix. For the people of Russia the city was like a burning bush from which the voice of the country's destiny was to be heard in days of great sorrow and rejoicing.

The earliest mention of Moscow is to be found in the Nikonian Chronicle which cites a missive from Yury Dolgoruky (George of the Long Arm), the youngest son of Vladimir Monomakh and the appanage prince of the lands of Suzdal, exhorting Svyatoslav, Prince of Novgorod-Seversky, to join him. The invitation, full of elation from a recent victory over the host of Ryazan, elicited a similar response from Svyatoslav, who had triumphed in the intestine skirmishes within the ranks of Smolensk. Dolgoruky wrote: "Come to me, brother, to Moscow... With respectful greetings for the Friday of Thanksgiving to the Mother of God." On 18 March 1147, the allied princes and their retinues gathered for a "great feast" and everyone "rejoiced together."

During the reign of Yury Dolgoruky, Moscow was a trading village with extensive land for grazing and farming and dwellings to house the prince and his soldiers and servants. The choice of location was influenced by the practicality of the hilly surroundings and the proximity of rivers and a thick pine forest. Bordered by the River Moscow and the mouth of the River Neglinnaya, the promontory on which Moscow stood not only boasted strong natural defences, but also imparted that certain magnetism that is peculiar to great cities to the settlement that grew up there. Here, most likely at the beginning of the 10th century, members of the East Slavic tribe of the Viatichi and other brave people had settled in the knowledge that the site on Borovitsky Hill (where the Kremlin stands today) could become a key link in the routes leading through the Russian principalities to the east as well as to the heart and the north of Ancient Rus'. All of these factors contributed to the transformation of Moscow from a princely village into a city guarded by a fortress, the Kremlin.

Yury Dolgoruky built many towns as strategic sites to protect the lands of Vladimir and Suzdal, but Moscow remained his favourite. In 1156, the prince ordered that Borovitsky Hill be surrounded by a fortification or *gorod* (from which the Russian word for "city" originates), consisting of a bank of earth and a system of wooden defences. Trading quarters sprung up around the Kremlin and the centre of what was then an appanage principality began to take shape.

Following in the ancestral tradition of the House of Rurik, each prince made his own material and spiritual contribution to the development of the city, adding his personal touch to the common canvas. Moscow achieved particular fame under Alexander Nevsky's fourth son, who was christened in honour of St. Daniel the Stylite in 1261. After his father's death in 1263, Daniel became the nominal head of the principality, but did not rule independently until 1276 (in the meantime, Grand Prince Yarolsav of Vladimir ruled in his name). In 1305, Daniel died "on his ancestral estate in Moscow a member of the monastic order," i.e., having taking his vows and been absolved of his sins. After Daniel's death, his son Yury came to the throne. When Yury was murdered in 1325, his brother Ivan assumed leadership of the principality of Moscow. Ivan was nicknamed Kalita ("moneybag"), reflecting his policy of "gathering" the Russian principalities into a single empire and augmenting the public coffers.

In 1337–38, during Ivan Kalita's reign, Moscow was sacked and burnt by the Horde of Batu Khan. Natural fires, which occasionally engulfed the entire city, also posed a continual threat to the growth of Moscow. The first of such fires occurred in the summer of 1331 and was followed by similar incidents in 1335 and 1337. Yet Moscow recovered again and again. Towards the end of Kalita's life, the original cathedrals of the Dormition and the Archangel Michael were erected along with a royal mansion and the Palace of the Metropolitan. The Kremlin was fortified with sturdy oak walls. Ivan I made Moscow the strongest of the principalities of Rus' while at the same time establishing his authority over many towns and exerting an active influence on Novgorod. Under Kalita, Moscow became the spiritual centre of Rus', a fact that was confirmed by the transfer of Metropolitan Peter, the head of the Russian Orthodox Church, from Vladimir to Moscow.

The culmination of the rise of Moscow came during the reign of Dmitry (1359–1389), son of Ivan the Meek and grandson of Ivan Kalita. Moscow's achievements had been so great and distinct under the rule of the Rurik dynasty that the Muscovites defended Dmitry's right to princehood before the Horde, despite the fact that he was still a boy. Their hopes were justified, for Dmitry often displayed wisdom and courage. He succeeded in retaining the title of Grand Prince from the Horde as well as having the town of Vladimir recognised as the hereditary property of the princes of Moscow and the status of the princes of Tver reduced to the level of appanage, i.e., subordinate to Moscow. Having survived defeat by the troops of the Horde in 1377, Dmitry crushed them the following year. The grand prince consolidated this victory at the Battle of Kulikovo on 8 September 1380. Two armies of one hundred thousand men apiece met at the point where the River Nepryadva flows into the Don. On the one side was the army

of Khan Mamai and on the other, the Russian army led by Dmitry and inspired by the parting words and blessing of St Sergius of Radonezh, the founder of the Holy Trinity Monastery. The victory on Kulikovo Field became the most powerful spiritual boost to the subsequent and final liberation of Rus' from the Mongol-Tatar yoke. Although Khan Tokhtamysh succeeded in temporarily seizing power over Moscow in 1382 by means of deceit, Dmitry, nicknamed Donskoy, secured Moscow's position as the capital of the grand principality, and after his death the throne passed by succession to his son, Vasily I.

Dmitry Donskoy had dedicated himself to the task of fortifying, improving and embellishing the Kremlin. During his reign, white stone walls punctuated with towers were erected together with new mansions and stone churches. Now that it had been rebuilt in stone, the Kremlin emphasised Moscow's pre-eminence over all the towns of Rus'.

Vasily I maintained the tradition that had been set by his predecessors, annexing new territory, reducing neighbouring principalities to the level of administrative districts and consolidating the power of the grand prince who became the supreme military commander. The conqueror of North Asian countries, Timur (Tamerlane), tried to put a stop to the rise of Moscow, but having stood for two weeks on the Ryazan frontier, his troops retreated, unwilling to fight the Russian army. For a while, Rus' ceased to render tribute to the Horde, which inevitably affected the physical development of Moscow. In 1408, the Mongol-Tatar warriors fell upon Rus' in their thousands, sacking such significant towns as Rostov and Nizhny Novgorod. Although the emir, Edygei, did not succeed in storming Moscow, the Muscovites agreed to recognise his authority and paid him a pecuniary tribute in order to avoid further bloodshed. Having been saved, Moscow continued to expand and grow in strength and beauty.

The reign of Ivan III was marked by one of the most major historical phenomena: in 1476, Moscow paid tribute to the Horde for the last time. In 1480, Khan Akhmat led his army of one hundred thousand men against Rus' in the hope of punishing it. When he was met by the Russian host at the Ugra River, the khan realised that he was in danger of suffering a terrible defeat and withdrew. So ended the Mongol-Tatar yoke. At the end of the 15th century, the name Russia gained a foothold. At official functions Ivan III was addressed as Tsar of All Rus' and bore the symbols of an autocrat: the grand princely crown (the Cap of Monomakh), a sumptuous shoulder mantle and a sceptre and orb. The national coat of arms depicting the double-headed eagle officially came into use. Moscow prevailed over a vast territory with a population of several million, which in turn made it possible to solve the serious town-planning issues with which the expanding city was faced.

Between 1485 and 1495, by order of Ivan III, the white stone of the walls and towers of the Kremlin was replaced with red brick, interspersed with white stone foundations and details. Alterations were made to the cathedrals of the Dormition and the Annunciation, the foundations were laid for the Archangel Cathedral and the Faceted Palace was built. The grounds of the Kremlin were also enlarged somewhat and assumed the boundaries and configuration that are to be seen today.

The dominant position of the Kremlin and its circular outline influenced the design of the rest of Moscow for centuries to come. The layout of the city is essentially reminiscent of the spreading rays of the sun, intersected by a series of rings. From the very early years of its existence and throughout the reign of Moscow's Rurik dynasty from Daniel to Fyodor, the Kremlin assumed an important role as a hub of spiritual and state power and also as a centre of Russian culture. The appearance of the Kremlin with its crenellated walls invokes the image of an ancient crown and indeed it crowns Moscow, towering above the River Moscow and the capital's central square, the famous Red Square. The walls of the Kremlin are punctuated with towers, making it all the more imposing and impregnable. Its infrangibility is reflected in the very word "kremlin," derived from *kremen'* (flint).

A symbol of the Kremlin and its history is the Saviour (Spasskaya) Tower. Its importance was emphasised by special inscriptions in Old Russian and Latin. The name, which dates back many centuries, is linked to a legend in which a nun of the Ascension Convent saw the image of the Mother of God and the saints of Moscow in a prophetic dream, imploring the people not to surrender the city to the Tatar khan. In answer to the supplications of all the inhabitants of Moscow, the aggressor withdrew without a fight. That was in 1521. In commemoration of the miraculous salvation of the city, an image of Christ the Saviour was painted over the gates overlooking Red Square and in 1658 the tsar ordered that the gate and tower be officially named in memory of this extraordinary event.

Cathedral Square represents the spiritual, ideological and artistic nucleus of the Kremlin ensemble. The atmosphere of the square is rich in the great sentiments of public joy and woe. Here the dominant church building is a cathedral dedicated to the great event in Christian history of the Dormition of the Virgin. Crowned with five cupolas that are reminiscent of the golden helmets of the heroes of epic Russian folktales, the Dormition Cathedral seems monolithic. Its artistic design combines elements of Old Russian and Renaissance architecture. The interior of the cathedral, with its splendid murals and the glimmering frames of its ancient icons, is like a wondrous celestial boat intended to transport the faithful to the most lofty heights.

In front of the Kremlin lies the broad expanse of Red Square, the Russian name for which also means beautiful. Although the square has had many names over the years, its current title was officially adopted in the 19th century. Red Square is the site of the Cathedral of the Intercession, better known as the Church of St Basil the Blessed, which sparkles playfully like a rare and exquisite jewel. The church's ten domed and peaked roofs are like the flames of fantastic candles and its radiant quality is further enhanced by the extremely diverse use of coloured tiles. Over the centuries, the Cathedral of the Intercession has lost none of its deeply spiritual significance as a symbol of nationwide supplication and exultation. It is no coincidence that the church is flanked by a monument commemorating one of the key events in Russian history, namely the liberation of Moscow from the Polish enemy in 1612 through the efforts of Russia's volunteer army led by Kuzma Minin, a butcher from Nizhny Novgorod, and Prince Dmitry Pozharsky. Erected in 1818, the monument not only became an organic part of the majestic architectural symphony of the Kremlin and its neighbouring square, but also evoked memories of the heroism of the Russian army in the Patriotic War of 1812.

All of the stylistic changes that bear witness to the key stages in the development of European art are clearly reflected in the face of Moscow. Apraksin House is an outstanding example of the architectural tastes of the mid-18th century, when the Baroque style was prevalent. The Catherine Palace, built for Admiral Golovin in 1773–96, serves as the antithesis to the decorative splendour of the Baroque. A slightly younger contemporary of the Catherine Palace is Pashkov House (1784–86). Erected on Vagankovsky Hill, it overlooks the Kremlin. The man behind this piece of architectural genius was Vasily Bazhenov. The artistic refinement of Bazhenov's creation later decided its future: in 1861, a priceless collection of books and other works belonging to Nikolay Rumyantsev was brought here, laying the foundations for the Public Library. Pashkov House is just one example of the masterpieces of so-called classical Moscow. The author of its greatest achievements, however, was Matvey Kazakov. A classical architect, he created the Peter Stopover Palace, commissioned by Catherine II. Although the layout of the palace is typically classical, its facade, designed and decorated in the pre-Petrine style, evokes memories of the Moscow of the 16th – 17th centuries. In the 1780s, the Noble Assembly, known as the House of Councils after the Revolution, was built to design by Kazakov. This building, which is of significance not only to Moscow but to the history of Russia too, boasts a magnificent Hall of Columns.

In the early 19th century, after Napoleon's army had been expelled from Moscow and the city had risen from the ashes, signs of the lifting of spirits experienced by all of Russian society and the people of the ancient capital in particular began to appear on the face of Moscow. Osip Bove became one of the individuals who lent the joy of victory physical expression in the city's architecture. The Theatre Square ensemble, comprising two theatre buildings, the Bolshoi and the Maly, was shaped according to his designs. The Bolshoi Theatre became the emblem of Russian achievement in opera and ballet and one of the most respected theatres in the world. The Tretyakov brothers, Pavel and Sergey, famous collectors of Russian art, presented Moscow with both an art gallery and an entire collection of works. The gallery's decorative main entrance was designed in the style of ancient Russian architecture by the artist Victor Vasnetsov: an intricate *kokoshnik* with a carved and gilded surround provides the backdrop for a relief of St George slaying the dragon. This symbol of Russia and Moscow reflects the significance of the collection itself – service to Russian art.

Following the shocks inflicted by the revolutions and the civil war and once Moscow had again been named the state capital, the appearance of the city began to undergo irreversible historic and artistic changes. One of the most tragic outcomes of these events was the destruction of many Orthodox places of worship, namely cathedrals and monasteries, as well as other old buildings. However, it should not be forgotten that the 1920s produced skilfully contrived and innovative works in the style of architectural Constructivism. Moscow grew upwards and outwards, an underground railway was built and monumental government buildings sprung up. Tall buildings topped with spires became a striking and lasting feature of the Moscow skyline. They introduced a new physical dimension into the capital, complementing and enriching the existing dynamism of the Kremlin churches and towers. In recent years Moscow's urban landscape has been actively developed: a large number of unique edifices, home to companies and corporations, hotel complexes and residential buildings have been created. The restoration of the Cathedral of Christ the Saviour has been a highly symbolic phenomenon in the history of Russia. The cathedral was originally built to commemorate Russia's victory in the Patriotic War of 1812, marking both the salvation of the country from the Napoleonic invasion and the part played by Moscow and its inhabitants, who shouldered most of the burden during the war. The Cathedral of Christ the Saviour became a Russian cultural monument and a majestic popular place of worship, adored by the people as a tangible expression of their faith, virtue and strength. On 19 August 2000, the Feast of the Transfiguration of Our Lord, the reconstructed cathedral was consecrated. In this unique historical event, Moscow and Russia were given back their most important cathedral, creating a bridge between the past and the present and opening new doors for future creative triumphs. The stellar light that surrounds Moscow has never once been extinguished. Today, at the beginning of the 21st century, the bells of the ancient cathedrals, restored to new life, can again be heard ringing out over "great and gold-domed" Moscow. This is the jubilant "voice of time" that resounds with the enormous energy and vigour of the past, while heralding the indubitable attainment of future heights. It is here in the voice of Moscow, as in its image as a whole, that Russia's underlying strength, its confidence in its ability to fulfil its difficult destiny and its bold and imaginative approach to the future lie hidden.

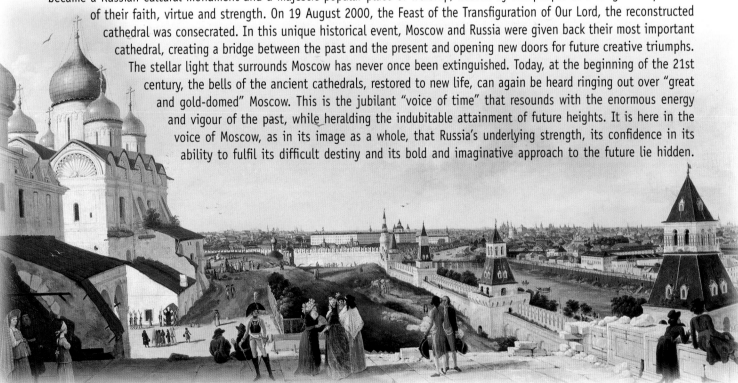

Kremlin

The Kremlin is Moscow's central architectural ensemble, the heart of Russia and symbol of its greatness. It was built on lofty Borovitsky Hill at the confluence of two navigable rivers – the Moscow and the Neglinnaya (put into a conduit in the course of sanitation work and the city centre reconstruction, in 1816–20). This is the oldest part of Moscow, that as far back as the 11th century was the site of the Slaviansky town and its first manuscript reference dates from 1147.

In the reign of Yury Dolgoruky, prince of Vladimir and Suzdal, it was surrounded by a moat with ramparts. In the early 14th century Moscow became capital of the principality with the white-stone Kremlin developing into an impregnable fortress.

1. View of the Kremlin from the Bolshoi Kamenny Bridge

2. Konstantino-Yeleninskaya, Nabatnaya and Spasskaya Towers. 1490s. Architect Pietro Antonio Solario. Hipped roofs added in the 17th century

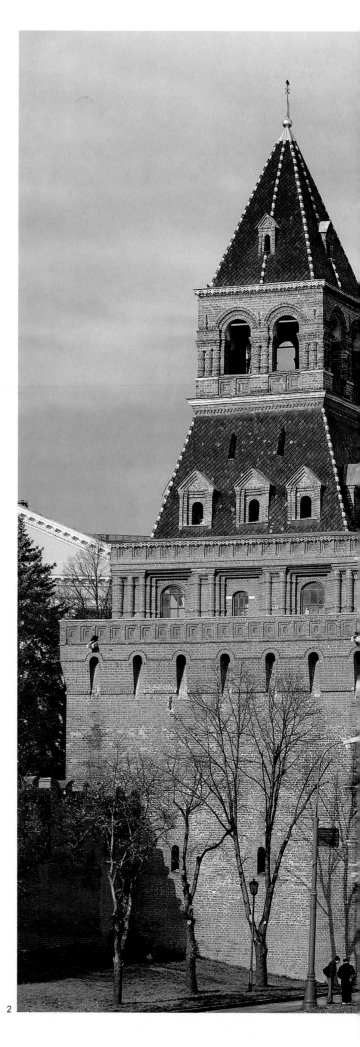

Towards the end of the 15th century, when the Moscow principality was transformed into the state of Muscovy, the Kremlin assumed a new significance, it was rebuilt and enlarged. It was then that the ensemble's style was mainly formed, its area of 27.5 hectares being enclosed with new mighty fortified structures. Majestic new cathedrals replaced the former white-stone churches on Sobornaya and Ivanovskaya Squares which seemed too small for the great capital, and the princes' and boyars' dwellings stretched from the slope of Borovitsky Hill to the western section of the fortified wall. This notable period of construction work was carried out by Italian architects invited to Russia by Ivan III. They included Aristotele Fioravanti, Alovisio di Carcanno, Marco Ruffo, Pietro Solario and Antonio Gilardi. The Italian masters succeeded in creating essentially Russian forms of church architecture that served as models for subsequent construction over the following two centuries.

Further development of the Kremlin as an ideological, political and cultural centre was impelled by the growth and territorial expansion of the capital. Intensive building in the 17th century transformed the Kremlin, giving it the characteristics we see today. The Terem Palace and its churches, the Poteshny (Amusement) Palace (site of first theatrical performances in Russia) and the Patriarch Courtyard with the Cathedral of the Twelve Apostles were erected, and the towers were topped with many-tier hipped roofs. In the 18th and 19th centuries major construction and reconstruction work was carried out in the palace complex and the state administration buildings: the Arsenal, Grand Kremlin Palace, Senate and Armoury all date from the period. The best Russian architects participated in it – Bartolommeo Rastrelli, Nikolay Lvov, Vasily Bazhenov, Matvey Kazakov, Konstantin Thon and Carlo Rossi.

In the Soviet epoch the Monastery of the Miracle (Chudov) and the Ascension Convent were demolished together with a great number of churches. The Palace of Congresses was built next to the Patriarch Palace between 1959 and 1961.

The imposing fortified structures of the Moscow Kremlin are best examples of mediaeval European fortifications. They were erected between 1485 and 1495 by the Italian architects and engineers Marco Ruffo, Antonio Gilardi, Pietro Antonio and Alovisio Antonio Solario. The vast territory of the Kremlin has the shape of an irregular triangle. The fortress walls have an overall length of 2,235 m. Along the perimeter stand nineteen fortified towers, with the Kutafya Tower overlooking

3. Spasskaya (Saviour) Tower. 1491.
Architect Pietro Antonio Solario; 1624–25. Architect B. Ogurtsov. Clockwork design by Christofer Halloway

4. Tsarskaya and Spasskaya Towers

5. Ruby star

It is the most beautiful tower of all those surrounding the main Russian citadel. It was through the Spasskaya Tower that the Russian tsars used to enter the Kremlin. Colourful religious processions on the feast-days of the Kremlin churches and cathedrals also started here, the tradition having been recently revived. The tower got its name "Spasskaya" (Saviour) from

6

the Troitsky Bridge across the River Neglinnaya. Faced with large, well-baked bricks weighing 8 kg each, the walls are from 5 to 19 m high depending on the relief detail, and from 3.5 to 6.5 m thick as far as the merlons. Multi-tier towers, originally crowned with flat platforms for accurate aim in the traditional manner of European fortresses, were elevated with the addition of tall hipped roofs in the 17th century. The Spasskaya (Saviour) and Troitskaya (Trinity) towers are the tallest. The height of the Spasskaya Tower from its foundation up to the star atop its roof is 67.3 m.

6. Beklemishevskaya (Moskvoretskaya) Tower.
1487. Architect Marco Friazin

7. Nabatnaya Tower. 1490s.
Architect Pietro Antonio Solario

8. Troitskaya Tower. 1495. Kutafya Tower.
1516. Architect Alovisio Friazin

8

7

19

9

11

9. Vodovzvodnaya (Sviblova) Tower. 1488.
Architect Antonio Friazin.
Blagoveshchenskaya Tower. 1487–88 (?)

10. View of the Troitskaya Tower

11. View of Red Square from the Spasskaya Tower

12. Konstantino-Yeleninskaya, Nabatnaya
and Tsarskaya (1680s) Towers

the Image (icon) "Not-Made-by-Hands" of the Saviour placed above the gate which was considered almost "holy." The tower is crowned with a five-pointed ruby star set up there in 1937, it is similar to the stars atop four other Kremlin towers. The tower's major attraction is its bell chimes installed in three out of its ten tiers. They were cast by Russian craftsmen in the 17th – 18th centuries. The Kremlin clock shows the most accurate time in the country, being connected by an underground cable to the control system in the Institute of Astronomy.

13. Cupolas of the Upper Saviour Cathedral (1679–81)

Cathedral of the Dormition

Sobornaya (Cathedral) Square is the oldest in Moscow. Wooden churches first built there were later replaced with white-stone cathedrals of the same names put up on the same sites. The extant architectural ensemble adorning the square mainly formed in the late 15th – early 16th centuries, when Moscow was turning into the capital of the Russian state. That's why Sobornaya Square is justifiably considered a symbol of the unification of the Russian lands with Moscow as its centre.

The Cathedral of the Dormition used to be Russia's main cathedral.

14

15

Its construction and further reconstruction works always marked some crucial moments in Russia's history. It was founded in the early 14th century when Moscow princes just began to unify the Russian lands and Ivan Kalita was

←
14. Cathedral of the Dormition. Icon: The Fiery Eye of the Saviour. 1340s. From the Local Saints tier of the iconostasis

←
15. Cathedral of the Dormition. 1475–79. Architect Aristotele Fioravanti

←
16. Cathedral of the Dormition. Iconostasis. 1653

17. Cathedral of the Dormition. Icon of the Mother of God "Of the Sign". Vault painting. 17th century

18. Cathedral of the Dormition. Forty Martyrs of Sebastia. Fresco in the side chapel dedicated to the Apostles Peter and Paul. Late 15th – early 16th century. Detail

19. Cathedral of the Dormition. Interior

20

21

28

22

competing for the title and rights of grand prince. It was then that at the highest point of Kremlin Hill there was laid the foundation of a white-stone church dedicated, like the main cathedral in the city of Vladimir, to the Dormition of the Mother of God. The extant Dormition Cathedral was built in 1475–79 on the site of the original white-stone church by order of Ivan III. Though the cathedral was designed by the Italian architect and engineer Aristotele Fioravanti, its style and composition is consistent with the strict rules of the Orthodox canon.

Fragments of the original frescoes painted by a team of artists working under the guidance of the famous Russian icon-painter Dionysius have been preserved in the sanctuary (chancel). Other frescoes were executed in the 17th century by masters from various Russian towns, led by the court icon-painters Ivan and Boris Paisein.

The south, north and west walls are lined with the tombs of metropolitans and patriarchs. The heads of the Russian Orthodox Church had been buried here until 1721, when Peter the Great abolished the patriarchate and introduced administration by the Synod. The remains of the first metropolitan of Moscow lie in the north Sanctuary of St Peter. Metropolitan Peter

20. Cathedral of the Dormition.
Frescoes of the iconostasis. Late 15th century

21. Cathedral of the Dormition.
Icon by Dionysius (?) (c. 1440 – after 1502/3):
Metropolitan Peter with Scenes from His Life.
Late 15th – early 16th century

22. Cathedral of the Dormition. Vladimir Icon
of the Mother of God with Gospel episodes and
portraits of Church fathers in the borderscenes.
First quarter of the 16th century

23. Cathedral of the Dormition.
Icon of St George. 12th century. Novgorod

24. Cathedral of the Dormition.
Gospel. 1499. Moscow
"Small Zion" (tabernacle).
1486. Moscow

founded the metropolitan cathedra (chair) in the new Russian capital and initiated construction of the first white-stone Cathedral of the Dormition in 1326. An icon preserved in the cathedral portrays Metropolitan Peter in the centre and episodes from his life in borderscenes, including the erection of the cathedral.

The most important state ceremonies were held in the Cathedral of the Dormition: ordination of metropolitans and patriarchs, coronation of tsars and later emperors and public proclamation of state edicts.

During its existence the cathedral was decorated with the finest examples of ancient Russian art, in particular icons from the 12th to 17th centuries. Works of art collected by the grand princes, tsars, metropolitans and patriarchs formed the basis of the state treasury: priceless manuscripts

25

26

30

27

29

and art objects fashioned from gold and silver and decorated with precious stones that were crafted by the best painters, jewellers, engravers, metalworkers and gilders. After the closure of the cathedral in 1919 most of the collection was transferred to the Armoury, and many icons to the Tretyakov Gallery.

25. Cathedral of the Dormition. Prayer place of the tsarina. 17th century. Altered in the 19th century

26. Cathedral of the Dormition. Royal place of Ivan the Terrible. 1551

27. Cathedral of the Dormition. Icon by Dionysius (?) (c. 1440 – after 1502/3): Metropolitan Peter with Scenes from His Life. Late 15th – early 16th century. Detail

28, 29. Cathedral of the Dormition. Iron canopy set above the tomb of Patriarch Hermogenes. 17th century

*30. Religious
service at the walls
of the Dormition
Cathedral*

Cathedral of the Annunciation

The Cathedral of the Annunciation was built in 1485–89 as the domestic church of the tsars and grand princes of Muscovy. It was included in the complex of royal residences and palace buildings. The cathedral stands on the basement of an ancient 14th-century church. It was here that the tsar and his family celebrated christenings, weddings and daily prayers.

The interior is richly decorated. The cathedral contains frescoes painted

32

31. Cathedral of the Annunciation.
View of the iconostasis

32. Cathedral of the Annunciation.
Icon by Andrey Rublev (c. 1360/1370 – 1430s):
Annunciation. First half of the 15th century.
From the Feast tier of the iconostasis

33. Cathedral of the Annunciation. 1485–89

33

in 1508 by a team of court painters headed by Theodosius, son of the famous Dionysius. After the fire in 1547 Novgorod and Pskov masters repainted the damaged frescoes. The vivid, intense colourscale matches that of the luxurious royal chambers linked to the cathedral by special passageways. Painted on the vaults of the galleries is *The Tree of Jesse* composition, the Biblical genealogy of Jesus Christ, which also includes the figures of some prophets and classical philosophers. Next to their representations

35

37

36

34. Cathedral of the Annunciation.
Deesis tier of the iconostasis. Detail

35, 36. Cathedral of the Annunciation. *Details of the interior*

37. Cathedral of the Annunciation. *Iconostasis
in the side chapel dedicated to the Synaxis of the Archangel Gabriel*

37

38,39. Cathedral of the Annunciation. Frescoes. 1508

40. Cathedral of the Annunciation. Icon by Andrey Rublev
(c. 1360/1370 – 1430s): Transfiguration. 1405.
From the Feast tier of the iconostasis

41. Cathedral of the Annunciation. Altar crosses. 16th century

42. Cathedral of the Annunciation.
"Thin Candle" (candle holder). 17th century

40

are the portraits of first Moscow princes. Paintings on the pillars show the genealogical tree of Moscow tsars. The wall frescoes depict scenes from the Revelation to John, or Apocalypse of John, a New Testament book which tells of the end of this world and the Last Judgement. The many-tier gilded iconostasis is of great historical and artistic value. Its Deesis and Feast tiers are composed of icons from the late 14th – early 15th centuries. A number of them was painted by Andrey Rublev and Theophanes the Greek, the renowned master icon-painters of the late 14th and early 15th centuries. The sumptuousness of the royal cathedral is embellished by cast iron doors. The magnificent floor is inlaid with tiles of agate jasper.

41

42

Cathedral of the Archangel Michael

The cathedral which served as the burial place of the grand princes and tsars of Muscovy stands on the site of an ancient church built in the early 14th century and dedicated to the Archangel Michael, a guardian angel of the Moscow princes in war time. The present-day cathedral was erected between 1505 and 1508 by the Venetian architect Alovisio Novo and painted by the best masters

43. Cathedral of the Archangel Michael. Icon of the Archangel Michael. First third of the 15th century. From the Local Saints tier of the iconostasis

44. Cathedral of the Archangel Michael. 1505–08. Architect Alovisio Novo

45. Cathedral of the Archangel Michael. View of the iconostasis
→
46. Cathedral of the Archangel Michael. Interior

44

from Moscow, Yaroslavl and Kostroma: Yakov Kazanets, Stepan Rezanets, Simon Ushakov, Iosif Vladimirov, Gury Nikitin, Fyodor Zubov and others. Their paintings are most noteworthy. Compositions on the cathedral's south and north walls illustrate the deeds of the Archangel Michael and his heavenly host. The lower part of the walls contain the full-length portraits of the grand and appanage princes buried in the cathedral, while the frescoes on the pillars show their ancestors: Grand Prince Vladimir who converted Russia to Christianity, Princess Olga, his grandmother, Princes Andrey Bogolyubsky, Alexander Nevsky and his son Daniel, the forefather of the Moscow ruling dynasty. This arrangement of the frescoes personified the idea of grand princes being patronized by God and His saints. The "portrait gallery" of the cathedral comprises representations of more than sixty historical persons.

A tall four-tier iconostasis was installed here in the second half of the 16th century. Its Local Saints tier contains the main icon of the cathedral – that of the Archangel Michael with his deeds – from the late

47

48

47, 48. Cathedral of the Archangel Michael. Frescoes. 1564–65

49. Cathedral of the Archangel Michael. Iconostasis. 1679–81

14th – early 15th century, a rare example of icon-painting from the time of the Kulikovo Battle. The story of the icon is rather interesting. It was commissioned after the death of Grand Prince Dmitry Donskoy by his widow Princess Eudocia who wanted to commemorate her husband and the victory of the Russian army led by Dmitry at the Battle of Kulikovo.

All the grand princes and tsars prior to Peter the Great are buried in the cathedral which is crowded with the tombs of the members of the Rurik and Romanov dynasties. Ivan Kalita was the first to be interred in a small church located on the site of the present cathedral. The remains of Dmitry Donskoy were also placed there. When a new cathedral was constructed,

all the tombs of grand princes were transferred into it. The sarcophagi of the Rurik princes are arranged along the cathedral walls in a certain order. The graves of the Moscow grand princes are mainly to be found near the south wall, appanage princes, close relatives of the Moscow grand princes, are buried along the west wall, while the princes that fell into disgrace or were killed lie near the north wall. To the right of the iconostasis' holy doors, on a platform, there are the tombstones of Ivan III and Vasily III. The grandson of the former and son of the latter Tsar Ivan IV the Terrible with his sons are buried in the south part of the sanctuary. A special shrine was set up for them due to the fact that Ivan the Terrible had been the first to receive the title of tsar. Their tombs were opened in 1963 for archaeological research and the celebrated anthropologist Mikhail Gerasimov reconstructed the appearance of Tsars Ivan the Terrible and his son Fyodor Ivanovich. A carved white-stone canopy by the south-east pillar marks the grave of Tsarevich Dmitry, the youngest son of Ivan the Terrible, murdered at the age of eight

51

50. Cathedral of the Archangel Michael.
Funerary vessels. 16th century. From the grave
of Ivan the Terrible and his sons

51. Cathedral of the Archangel Michael.
Chalice and censer. 16th century.
Donations of Tsarina Irina Godunova

in 1591 and soon sanctified as a holy martyr.
The graves of the Romanov dynasty are near
the pillars of the cathedral's central part.
There are 56 graves and 46 tombstones in
the Cathedral of the Archangel Michael.

A distinguishing feature of its exterior
is its cupolas. It still remains an unsolved
mystery why only the central cupola of the
cathedral is gilded.

Church of the Deposition of the Robe

The domestic church of Russian metropolitans and patriarchs stands by the west portal of the Dormition Cathedral. It was built by Pskov architects between 1484 and 1486 in the style of early Moscow architecture. Rebuilding in the 16th to 18th centuries resulted in a number of alterations, but restoration work conducted from the 1930s to 1960s has reinstated the church's original appearance.

According to tradition, the robe of the Mother of God was brought to Constantinople from Palestine in the 5th century. It was an object of great veneration believed to protect the city from its enemies. In Russia the feast of the Deposition of the Robe was widely celebrated.

The church's cosy interior is in tune with its purpose. The frescoes preserved inside were painted by the court masters Ivan Borisov, Sidor Pospeyev, Semyon Avraamov in 1643–44. They illustrate the life-story of the Mother of God. The pillars supporting the vaults and the dome contain the representations of metropolitans and most venerated princes canonized by the Church. Here the visitor can see the figure of the youngest son of Ivan the Terrible Prince Dmitry murdered in Uglich. The sanctuary of the church is hidden behind the tall iconostasis. The icons are of an earlier date, completed by the patriarchal icon-painter Nazary Istomin in 1627. They include *The Trinity* and the *Mother of God with the Child*. The name of the painter of the church's main icon depicting the Deposition of the Robe and dating from the 17th century is unknown.

The holy doors used to belong to another church – the Saviour Church "in-the-Bor" situated next to the Grand Kremlin Palace. After the demolition of that

53

52. *Church of the Deposition of the Robe. 1484–86*

53. *Church of the Deposition of the Robe. Interior*

54

ancient structure the doors were transferred to the Church of the Deposition of the Robe.

A collection of Russian woodcarving from the 16th to 18th centuries is also preserved here. It is unique because most of the wooden sculpture has been destroyed by numerous fires. The oldest object on display is *St George the Warrior* that dates from the late 14th – early 15th century. Most noteworthy among 17th-century works are *St Nicholas of Mozhaisk* and the relief *Crucifixion with the Two Thieves*.

The Church of the Deposition of the Robe became part of the royal palace complex after the construction of the new patriarchal Church of the Twelve Apostles in the mid-17th century.

55

54. Church of the Deposition of the Robe.
Icon: Deposition of the Robe of the Mother of God. *17th century*

55. Church of the Deposition of the Robe. Holy doors. *15th century*

56. Church of the Deposition of the Robe. Frescoes. *1644*

Patriarch Palace
and the Church
of the Twelve Apostles

By the north facade of the Dormition Cathedral stands the Patriarch Courtyard complex. It was built under Patriarch Nikon who ordered extensive replacement and partial reconstruction of the older buildings in the mid-1650s. It was as spacious and luxurious as the Palace of the Tsar Alexey Mikhailovich. The ground floor housed various services, the second floor

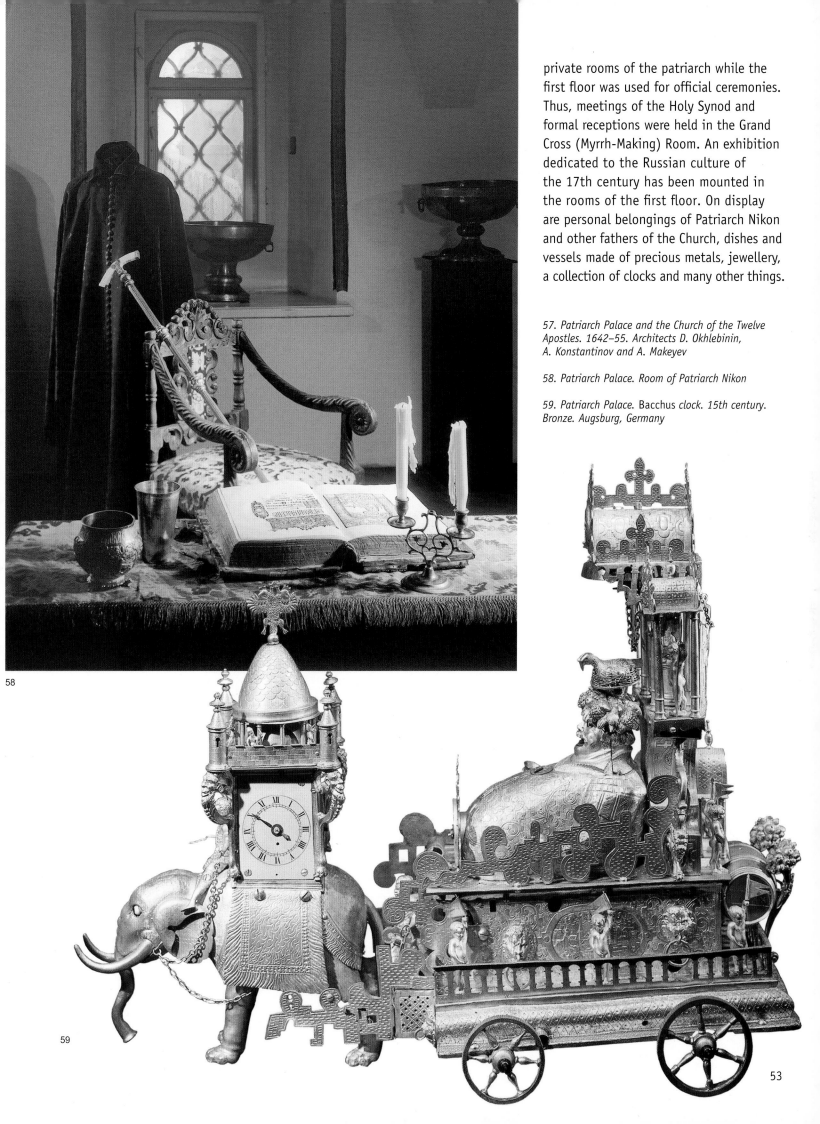

private rooms of the patriarch while the first floor was used for official ceremonies. Thus, meetings of the Holy Synod and formal receptions were held in the Grand Cross (Myrrh-Making) Room. An exhibition dedicated to the Russian culture of the 17th century has been mounted in the rooms of the first floor. On display are personal belongings of Patriarch Nikon and other fathers of the Church, dishes and vessels made of precious metals, jewellery, a collection of clocks and many other things.

57. Patriarch Palace and the Church of the Twelve Apostles. 1642–55. Architects D. Okhlebinin, A. Konstantinov and A. Makeyev

58. Patriarch Palace. Room of Patriarch Nikon

59. Patriarch Palace. Bacchus clock. 15th century. Bronze. Augsburg, Germany

58

59

53

The new domestic church, the Church of the Twelve Apostles, was erected above the gateway leading to the Patriarch Courtyard. Its gilded carved decor dating from the late 17th century is a fine sample of the Moscow Baroque style.

In 1505–08 a bell tower, some 60 m high, was put up above the existing Church of St John Climacus which was accordingly named in honour of the saint: "Ivan (John) the Great." In 1600 the tower was extended to a height of 81 m. The Church with the Bell Tower of the Resurrection of Christ was added to the north flank between 1532 and 1534. It houses the largest bell in Russia still in working order – the Dormition, or Festive, Bell.

60. Church of the Twelve Apostles. Iconostasis. Transferred from the Church of the Ascension demolished in the Moscow Kremlin

61, 62. Patriarch Palace. Grand Cross (Myrrh-Making) Room. Exhibition of the Museum of the Applied Art and Life-Style of 17th-century Russia

61

62

63. Ivanovskaya Square

At the foot of the "Ivan the Great" bell tower there stands the so-called Tsar-Bell, the largest bell in the world. Its weight is 200 tons, its height 6.14 m and the diameter 6.6 m. Next to the Church of the Twelve Apostles there is the Tsar-Cannon, a wonder of 16th-century casting. Its weight is 40 tons, its length 5.34 m and the calibre 890 mm which was the largest for its time.

64. Architectural ensemble with "Ivan the Great" bell tower. 1505–08. Architect Bon Friazin; 1532–43. Architect P. Maly; 1600, 1624. Architect B. Ogurtsov

65. Ivanovskaya Square. Tsar-Cannon. 1586. Master A. Chokhov

66. Ivanovskaya Square. Tsar-Bell. 1733–35. Cast by I. and M. Motorin
→
67. Kremlin bells
→
68. Cupolas of the Kremlin cathedrals

Faceted Palace

The Faceted Palace is the oldest secular
building in Moscow. Constructed by order
of Ivan III it owes its name to the decorative stonework on its east facade. It was
part of the palace complex of grand princes and was used for ceremonial receptions.
Most important events in Russia's history
were marked here with festivities. Thus,
it was here that Ivan the Terrible celebrated his victory over the city of Kazan and
Peter I his victory over the Swedes in the
Battle of Poltava.

The interior of the Faceted Palace is
a spacious, almost square in form, hall
with a tetrahedral pillar in the centre supporting its cross-shaped vaults.

←
69. Faceted Palace. 1487–1591.
Architects Marco Ruffo and Pietro Antonio Solario

70. Faceted Palace. Red (Beautiful) Porch

71. Faceted Palace. First Rurik Princes.
Painting on the east wall. 1882.
By the Belousov brothers (Palekh)

*72. Faceted
Palace. Interior*

The original frescoes that once decorated the Faceted Palace have been destroyed. For the first time its interior was painted in the 16th century. Due to numerous fires, the Faceted Palace badly deteriorated in the mid-17th century and its decorations and frescoes needed renovation. They were restored by the Moscow icon-painter Simon Ushakov who also described all the subjects of the frescoes. The extant murals were done in 1883 in oil by the Belousov brothers, master craftsmen from the village of Palekh, who used in their work the descriptions of Simon Ushakov.

The carved white-stone porch, known as the Beautiful (or "Red" which had the meaning of "beautiful" in Slavonic) Porch, used to play an important ceremonial role as it led to the palace's Holy Entrance Hall which was linked to Tsarina's Golden Wing,

annexed to the palace in the 16th century. The documents call it the Golden Wing of Tsarina Irina, the spouse of Tsar Fyodor Ioannovich. It got its name from the fact that in the late 16th century all the paintings here were done against the golden background. The original frescoes have been restored through the efforts of experts and now we can enjoy their bright colourscale comprising yellow, green and white against the festive-looking golden background.

73. *Faceted Palace. Tsarina's Golden Wing.*
Entrance of St Dinara into Tabriz.
Fresco on the north wall. 17th century

74. *Faceted Palace. Tsarina's Golden Wing*

75. *Faceted Palace. Tsarina's Golden Wing. East wall*

76. *Faceted Palace. Holy Entrance Hall*

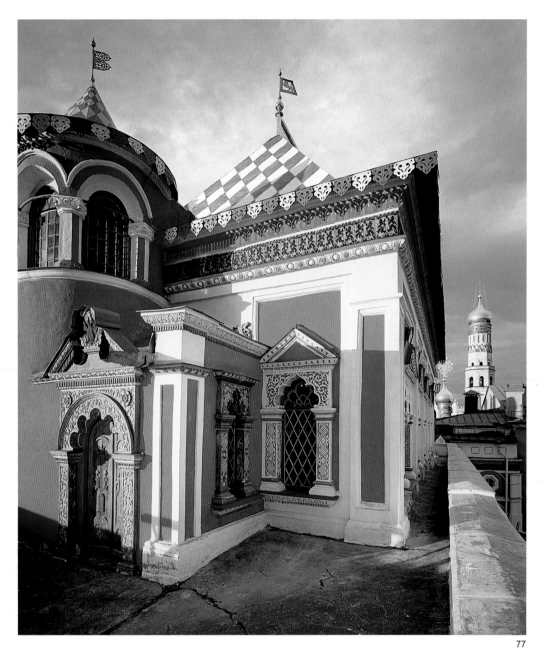

77

Terem Palace

77. Terem Palace. Golden-roofed
Teremok and Watch Tower

78. Terem Palace. 1635–36.
Architects B. Ogurtsov, L. Ushakov,
T. Sharutin and A. Konstantinov

When the Time of Troubles was over
and Tsar Michael Fyodorovich ascended the
throne, there arose a necessity to renovate
the royal residence demolished and burnt
by the Poles. The temporary palace put up
in 1614 was replaced in 1620 by another
one constructed by the royal carpenter
Isayev. But as fires were frequent in Moscow, the building of a new stone palace
was started by the masons Bazhen Ogurtsov,
Lazar Ushakov, Trifon Sharutin, Antip
Konstantinov and others. Its decoration
was completed in 1637. Its facades have
come to us almost unaltered. The structure
is based on three cubes placed one upon
another at some distance from their walls'
edges. The Late Gothic ornamentation

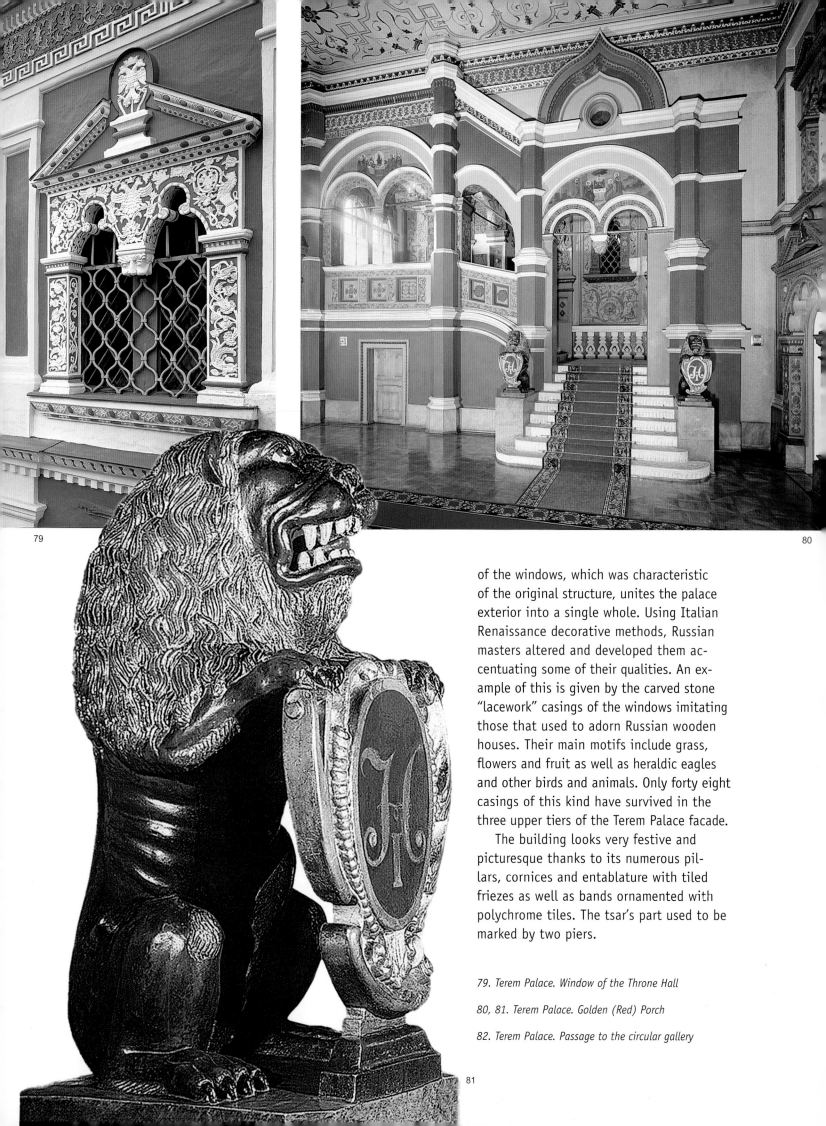

of the windows, which was characteristic of the original structure, unites the palace exterior into a single whole. Using Italian Renaissance decorative methods, Russian masters altered and developed them accentuating some of their qualities. An example of this is given by the carved stone "lacework" casings of the windows imitating those that used to adorn Russian wooden houses. Their main motifs include grass, flowers and fruit as well as heraldic eagles and other birds and animals. Only forty eight casings of this kind have survived in the three upper tiers of the Terem Palace facade.

The building looks very festive and picturesque thanks to its numerous pillars, cornices and entablature with tiled friezes as well as bands ornamented with polychrome tiles. The tsar's part used to be marked by two piers.

79. Terem Palace. Window of the Throne Hall

80, 81. Terem Palace. Golden (Red) Porch

82. Terem Palace. Passage to the circular gallery

83

The arch of the upper platform of the staircase has a boss with its end shaped as a stylized lion's head. It served as sort of talisman believed to protect the royal residence from evil forces. The lion holds in its mouth the "apple of silence" as if keeping all the royal affairs secret. As all the tsars wanted to emphasize the principle of royal succession, there are many representations of lions in the palace decor. A lion was a symbol of the ancient capital of Vladimir inherited by Moscow, the new capital of Russia.

The Terem Palace interiors comprised the Dining Room, Entrance and Throne halls, Bedroom and Prayer Room. The Dining Room (Refectory) was the first in the suite of royal apartments. Dinners for beggars and war prisoners were given here on the days of family celebrations or in commemoration of some important events. Later it was used for receptions, here the boyars were waiting for the entry of the tsar in the morning.

Next to it was the Entrance Hall, also called Duma or Council Hall as it was here that the tsar discussed various problems with the boyar council. The tsar would sit in his royal chair and the boyars on the benches along the walls. They heard trials and read petitions. It was here that the tsar made his decisions and announced his verdicts.

Next was the Throne Hall, or Tsar's Study, which has undergone certain alterations. Originally its vault had a painting of the Saviour and holy bishops while today there are only figures of saints in the cartouches. At the entrance there is a pair of the gilded statues of heraldic lions. The colour of the walls decorated with the golden emblems of Russian principalities and cities used to be bright red, now it is crimson. Dedicated to the glorious history of Russia, the Study had the golden emblems of all Russia's guberniyas (provinces). Its furnishings were rather simple. There stood oak tables and benches along the walls. The highlight of the room was the royal chair with a carpet before it which, according to tradition, was embroidered by the tsar's daughters.

In the second half of the 17th century the palace became the main residence of Russian tsars. On the lower floor there were service areas and kitchens, and on the first floor articles of ceremonial attire were made in the Workshop Room. The second floor was occupied by women's part, while the tsar's quarters took up the entire third floor. The palace interiors display a variety of fanciful ornaments and impress the visitor by their unusual planning. The Golden Porch would be the main entrance to the palace. Some of its gilding missing, it is still extremely beautiful.

83, 84. Terem Palace. Throne Hall

The window in the middle was known as the "petition window": a special box was lowered from it on the outside and everyone had the right to drop his petition addressed to the tsar into the box. The box was called "long" as the reading of the petitions took a very long time. The Study, like the Refectory, had elegant stoves richly ornamented with glazed tiles. The tiles usually displayed geometrical or floral patterns and seldom showed any subjects.

85. Terem Palace. Duma (Council) Hall

86. Terem Palace. Bedroom

87. Terem Palace. Entrance Hall.
Tiled stove. Detail

88

89

88. *Terem Palace. Golden (Red) Porch. Boss of the "Lion Mask" arch*

89. *Terem Palace. Throne Hall. Carved wooden window-sill*

90. *Terem Palace. Entrance Hall*

91. *Terem Palace. Prayer Room. Gilded carved icon cases. 18th century*

There was a flower or rosette in the centre, and the rest was filled with cartouches or curled stems.

The Study was followed by the Bedroom and then Prayer (Cross) Room. In the 17th century the latter contained most valuable old icons in gold and silver frames adorned with precious stones. Unfortunately the original murals of the Terem Palace have not survived, though it is known that they were done under

the guidance of the court icon-painter Simon Ushakov.

The Terem Palace was part of a large Tsar's Courtyard, a whole architectural complex which also included buildings for assemblies and receptions, palace churches, separate wooden palaces for the tsar, tsarina, their sons and daughters. All the structures were placed at different levels and linked with one another by passageways, inner courtyards and platforms.

Palace Cathedrals

92. Church of the Nativity of the Mother of God. Interior

93. Cupolas of the Upper Saviour Cathedral

Tsarina's Golden Wing is one of the Kremlin's highlights. It was put up in the reign of Tsar Fyodor Ioannovich for his wife Irina Godunova. The paintings of Tsarina's Wing are the only specimens of old secular murals. In 1636 a superstructure was added to the building to house the Upper Saviour Cathedral. In 1681 the Church of the Crucifixion was built above Tsarina's Wing. All Russian tsars were very pious. Such was

Alexey Mikhailovich who could pray for five hours running and make up to one thousand prostrations and sometimes more. The intensive religious life of the tsars made it necessary to annex churches to their palace. They were home churches of the tsars and their spouses and the royal court took special care of them. In the 17th century there were eleven churches in the palace.

The chief architect of the project was Konstantin Thon who later built the Cathedral of Christ the Saviour. He was concerned with planning, designed the palace facades and directed the construction work. Moscow architects N. Chichagov, F. Richter, N. Shokhin and P. Gerasimov also contributed to the project: they designed the interiors. As to the style of the Grand Kremlin Palace, it imitates and interprets the forms and decorative motifs of the Terem Palace. The revival of mediaeval Russian architectural tradition was in tune

Grand Kremlin Palace

The Faceted Palace, Holy Entrance Hall, Tsarina's Golden Wing and Terem Palace as well as the palace cathedrals and churches are parts of the imposing Grand Kremlin architectural ensemble made up of religious and secular structures. The idea of uniting several architectural structures from different epochs with one facade had no analogous in Russian architecture and was suggested by Emperor Nicholas I. The emperor wanted his Moscow residence to be full of splendour and grandeur, thus emphasizing the firmness of the Romanov dynasty's power.

The magnificent building of the Kremlin Palace was constructed on the site of ancient palace structures. It acquired its present-day appearance in 1838–50.

94. View of the Grand Kremlin Palace

95. Grand Kremlin Palace. 1838–50. Architect K. Thon

96

96. Grand Kremlin Palace. Dormer-window of the dome with bell chimes

97

with the slogan representing the guiding
principle of Nicholas I's reign: "Orthodoxy,
Autocracy and Nationality."

The palace has the shape of a square
and consists of 700 rooms with an area of
approximately 20,000 m². All the interiors
are noted for their sumptuous furnishing.
Service areas and private apartments
of the imperial family were situated

97. Grand Kremlin Palace.
Guards of Honour on the Main Staircase

98. Grand Kremlin Palace.
St George Hall. North-west door

on the ground floor. State rooms on the first floor are named after highest Russian decorations – orders of St George, St Vladimir, St Alexander and others.

To the right of the anteroom there is the most famous hall in the suite of state apartments dedicated to the Order of St George. It is considered "the largest and grandest hall" in Russia. By its enormous size (60 m long, 19 m wide and 17 m high) it surpasses all other "order" halls of the palace. Its harmonious proportions and impeccable style of the decor done in white and gold are stunning.

The hall has got its name from the Order of St George the Conqueror instituted by Catherine II in 1769. Its vaults are

99. *Grand Kremlin Palace. St George Hall.*
Minin and Pozharsky *chimney clock.*
Mid-19th century. Bronze.
After the model of the sculptor
A. Loganovsky

100. *Grand Kremlin Palace.*
St George Hall. St George
the Conqueror chimney clock.
Mid-19th century. Bronze.
After the model of the sculptor
A. Loganovsky

101. *Grand Kremlin Palace.*
St George Hall

100

102

supported by eighteen pylons. Their eighteen columns facing the central part of the hall are crowned with statues personifying the territories joined to the Russian Empire. The marble plaques on the walls contain the names of military units awarded by the Order of St George. The names of the knights of the Order are to be seen on the marble ribbons. There are two fireplaces made of Carrara marble with bronze clocks standing on them (near the longer walls). This gorgeous hall is lighted by six gilded bronze chandeliers, each weighing 1,300 kg. Noteworthy is the remarkable parquet floor composed of twenty different kinds of wood.

The St George Hall is a memorial of Russian military glory and a sort of monument to the courage and valour of Russia's people. It was by no chance that a celebration was arranged here to honour the participants of the Victory Parade of 1945.

In 1934 the St Alexander and St Andrew halls were dismantled and redesigned into

102. *Grand Kremlin Palace. St Alexander Hall*

103. *Grand Kremlin Palace. View of the St Andrew Room from the St Alexander Hall*

104. *Grand Kremlin Palace. St Andrew Hall*

an enormous Congress Hall where conferences and congresses of the Communist
Party used to be held. Today we can see
and appreciate the restored decor
of each of them.

The St Andrew Hall was the main
ceremonial room of the Moscow Kremlin.
By the decree of Emperor Nicholas I, it was
dedicated to the first order instituted

in Russia by Peter I which became the highest state award – the Order of St Andrew the First-Called. The ceiling of the hall rests on ten heavy supports that divide its space into three parts. The luxurious moulding and gilding of its decor remind of the imperial grandeur. Near the wall opposite the entrance there is the royal throne place shaped as a marquee, with three chairs. Placed above it is the ancient symbol of the "All-Seeing Eye" expanding the "beams of light" covered with thin gold leaf.

The St Alexander Hall is one of most lavish rooms in the Grand Kremlin Palace, incomparable in the variety of its forms to other interiors. Peter I intended to have instituted the Order of St Alexander Nevsky but it was done only in 1925 after his death by his widow Catherine I. The colours of the decor are, as in other rooms, prompted by the colours of the Order: white, silver and red. The walls and vaults are abundantly, yet tastefully embellished with representations of the badges and stars of this most popular Russian order.

According to the plan of Nicholas I, the Hall of the Order of St Vladimir Equal-to-the-Apostles was to link the imperial residence to 16th- and 17th-century buildings of the complex. The hall is located between the Faceted Palace, Tsarina's Golden Wing, the Terem Palace and St George Hall. As if meant to connect various historical epochs, it is designed in the style of historicism using forms and elements of ancient Russian and Byzantine architecture. Surrounded on all its sides by other rooms, the hall has no windows and light comes only from a lantern in the centre of its octahedral dome. This small and intimate apartment has a circular shape which makes it look harmonious. The decor is in the colours of St Vladimir's Order: gold, red and black.

Noteworthy is the fact that the Order of St Vladimir (2nd class), with its motto "Usefulness, Honour and Glory," was given to the architect of the Grand Kremlin Palace and Cathedral of Christ the Saviour Konstantin Thon.

106

105. Grand Kremlin Palace.
Ceiling of the St Vladimir Hall with representations of St Vladimir's Order badges

106. Grand Kremlin Palace. St Vladimir Hall

The Grand Kremlin Palace was undoubtedly one of the best imperial residences, convenient both for ceremonial receptions and private life. The Red Drawing Room (former Ceremonial Bedroom) designed in the Renaissance style is one of most splendid apartments in the palace.
The private apartments of the imperial family are also lavish, yet cosy and intimate at the same time. Such are the Reception Room and Boudoir of the empress as well as the Study and Reception Room of the emperor.

107. Grand Kremlin Palace.
Red Drawing Room

108. Grand Kremlin Palace.
Guests' Part. Green Room

109. Grand Kremlin Palace.
Reception Room of the empress

109

110, 113. *Grand Kremlin Palace. Reception Room
of the emperor. Details of its furnishing
(upholstery of the armchairs and sofa, mid-19th century,
Sapozhnikovs Factory, Moscow; table top with
Florentine mosaic, mid-19th century,
Peterhof Lapidary Works)*

111. *Grand Kremlin Palace.
Boudoir of the empress*

112. *Grand Kremlin Palace.
Study of the emperor*

111

110

114

Senate – the Residence of the Russian Federation President

114. Senate. 1776–87. Architect M. Kazakov

115. Senate. St Catherine Hall

The Senate building designed by the architect Matvey Kazakov was put up in the Kremlin by order of Catherine in 1787. Its construction took twelve years and the Senate moved there in July, 1790, after the decoration of the interiors had been completed. The architect brilliantly performed his task matching the Neoclassical structure and the mediaeval ensemble

116

117

of the Kremlin. In the last two centuries the interiors were altered many times, as a result the original design of the architect underwent serious changes. In 1994–96 the building was restored and reconstructed in accordance with Kazakov's drawings and other archival documents, so it has acquired its original appearance again. Nowadays the Kremlin Senate is the residence of the Russian Federation President.

The St Catherine Hall, the main room of the building, which has been thoroughly restored, is used for formal state ceremonies, summit talks, investitures and presentations of awards and prizes. The bronze allegorical statues of Russia and Justice symbolize the new road of the country. Next to them there are the basreliefs and high reliefs from Kazakov's lifetime.

The style of decoration of the President's study and library is austere and formal.

116. Senate. Library of Russia's President

117. Senate. South courtyard. Winter garden

118. Senate. Emblem Hall

119. Senate. Winter garden. Interior

118

120

120. Panoramic view of the Moscow Kremlin.
The State Kremlin Palace. 1961–69.
Architects M. Posokhin, A. Mdoyants and others

The library contains the books which the President and his staff use in their daily work as well as the books with autographs presented to the President by their writers. The first in the suite of formal rooms is the Emblem, or Ambassadorial, Hall where accreditation documents are handed to the President. The State Emblem of the Russian Federation is its major decorative motif. The red damask with embroidered golden eagles perfectly matches the white pilasters with their gilded capitals.

Winter gardens arranged inside classical half-rotundas built in the inner courtyards are the latest innovations in the Senate building. The trees, flowers and bushes made of coloured glass are in tune with the Neoclassical decor.

Passing through the gateway of the Troitskaya Tower the visitor can enter the State Kremlin Palace housing the Kremlin Theatre. Its severe facades, typical of the architecture of the 1960s, contrast with the style of the Moscow Kremlin ancient structures. Originally it was constructed for the Communist Party conferences and congresses, so its name was the Palace of Congresses. Nowadays theatre performances and concerts are given here. The palace contains 700 rooms and halls and its theatre auditorium has 6,000 seats. The stage is located beneath ground level, with the palace's foundation being 16 m deep under the ground. The State Kremlin Palace is linked by passages to the Grand Kremlin and Patriarch Palaces.

State Armoury Diamond Fund

This is the oldest museum in Russia since the collection was started by the grand princes of Muscovy in the 14th and 15th centuries long before the Armoury Palace itself was established. The Treasure House, the first depository for valuables, was built in the Kremlin in 1485.

121. *State Armoury. Banner with the Emblem of the Russian Empire. Royal sword, sheath and shield. Late 17th century. Moscow*

122. *State Armoury. 1844–51. Architect K. Thon*

123. *State Armoury. Easter egg commemorating the 300th anniversary of the Romanov dynasty. 1913. Master X. Wigström. Carl Faberge's firm, St Petersburg. Gold, enamel, ivory, diamonds and crystal Monomakh's cap. Late 13th – early 14th century. East*

122

123

124. State Armoury. Showcase with samples of Western European armour and arms

125. State Armoury. Exhibition of Western European silverware from the 13th to 19th centuries

126. State Armoury. Main entrance and staircase

127. State Armoury. Sabre in sheath. 1829. Master I. Bushuyev. Town of Zlatoust. Steel, bronze, wood and ivory; etching, casting, burnishing and gilding

127

126

129

*128. State Armoury.
Attributes of a warrior
in ancient Russia*

*129. State Armoury.
Smolensk Icon of the Mother
of God. Late 16th century.
Icon frame by the Armoury
master-craftsmen*

*130. State Armoury.
Ceremonial helmet of Tsar
Michael Fyodorovich. 1621.
Armoury master Nikita Davydov
Steel, gold, silk, pearls, precious
stones and enamel; forging,
engraving and gilding*

*131, 132. State Armoury.
Samples of Russian and
Western European arms*

131   132

Orders and decorations from the State Armoury
and Diamond Fund (Nos 133–143)

133. Charter, star and badge of St Vladimir's Order

134. Badge of St Alexander Nevsky's Order

135. Diamond epaulette

136. Star and ribbon of St Catherine's Order

137. Cover of the Charter of St George's Order

138. Star of the Order of St Andrew
the First-Called

139. Regalia of the Knights of Malta

140. Badges of all classes and ribbon
of St George's Order

141. Star, badges of all classes and ribbon
of St Vladimir's Order

142, 143. Badge and chain of the Order
of St Andrew the First-Called

137

138

139

140

141

142

143

145

The Armoury is first mentioned in
a chronicle dating from 1547. Originally
it was used not only as a treasure house
for valuable art objects but also as
a workshop where both ceremonial and
martial arms were produced. In addition
to the armourers there were engravers,
metalworkers, bone-carvers, gilders and
filigreeworkers. In the 18th century production ceased, and towards the beginning of the 19th century the Armoury
received the status of royal museum.
Nowadays this is one of the finest collections of Russian and foreign decorative and applied art from the 4th to early
20th centuries.

146

*144. State Armoury. Carriage
of Empress Elizabeth Petrovna. 1754.
Master A. Drilerosse. France.
Maple, bronze, velvet and iron;
carving, gilding and painting*

*145. State Armoury. Coronation dress
of Elizabeth Petrovna. 1742.
Russia. Silk, silver brocade and lace;
embroidery*

*146. Diamond Fund. Brooch
(holder for a small bouquet of flowers). C. 1770
Diamonds, emeralds and gold*

147

148

One of the most valuable pieces is famous Monomakh's cap, the crown of Russian tsars. According to legend Monomakh's cap was sent to the Russian grand prince by Byzantine Emperor Constantine Monomakh. Since 1547 it has been used to crown the Russian tsars.

The State Armoury holds pieces by jewellers from St Petersburg's firm of Carl Faberge. Its refined Easter eggs made the firm famous worldwide. Best samples of its production composed of precious stones and metals, decorated with ivory,

147. State Armoury. Throne chair of Paul I. 1797. Russia. Wood and velvet; carving, gilding and embroidery

148. State Armoury. Double throne (of Tsars Ivan Alexeyevich and Peter Alexeyevich). 1682–84. Workshops of the Moscow Kremlin Silver and wood; casting, chasing, carving, engraving and gilding

149. State Armoury. Ermine mantle, a major part of the imperial dress

150. State Armoury. Royal regalia of Russia

151. Diamond Fund. Diadem: Russian Beauty. 1987.
Diamonds, pearls and gold

152. Diamond Fund. Brooch. 1777.
Diamonds, rubies, gold and silver

153. State Armoury. Clock in the shape of an Easter
egg crowned with a bouquet. 1899. Master M. Perkhin.
Carl Faberge's firm, St Petersburg
Gold, diamonds, onyx and enamel

156

158

159

154. State Armoury. Easter egg. 1902.
Master M. Perkhin. Carl Faberge's
firm, St Petersburg. Gold, platinum,
diamonds, rubies and enamel

155. Diamond Fund. Brooch.
Second half of the 18th century

156. State Armoury. Easter egg
containing a model of the Standard
royal yacht. 1909. Carl Faberge's
firm, St Petersburg
Gold, platinum, diamonds, emeralds,
lapis lazuli, crystal and enamel

157, 159. State Armoury.
Collection of works of Russian
applied and decorative art
from the 19th to early 20th centuries

158. State Armoury. Easter egg
containing a model of the Alexander
Palace. 1908. Carl Faberge's firm,
St Petersburg. Jade, gold, platinum,
diamonds, rubies and enamel

160

161

162

163

164

mother-of-pearl and other materials are displayed in the museum.

The ground floor of the Armoury building houses the Diamond Fund of Russia established in 1922. Kept in it are unique precious stones and recognized masterpieces of the art of jewellery. The earliest items date from the 1750s – 1760s. These are magnificent hairpins, earrings and diadems. They are adorned with diamonds of extraordinary brilliance. Of great historical and artistic value are the Great Imperial Regalia fashioned by Jérémie Pauzier in 1762 for the Coronation of Catherine II. This unique set is renowned for its fine craftsmanship and elegant design.

160–162, 164. State Armoury. Items from the "Olympic Service". Early 19th century Sevres, France. Porcelain; gilding and painting

163. State Armoury. Reliquary and pyx 13th century. Limoges, France Gold and enamel; chasing and engraving

165. State Armoury. Dish. 1633–40.
Paris. Silver and gold; chasing.

166. State Armoury. Vessel
in the shape of a horseman
(equestrian portrait of Charles I).
Before 1647. Augsburg, Germany
Gold and silver; chasing

165

166

167

167. State Armoury.
Vessel in the shape of a snow leopard.
1600–1601; Pitcher. 1604–05. England.
Silver; chasing and gilding

168. State Armoury. Bowl. 1817. France
Silver; gilding and chasing

168

119

Red Square

169. Panoramic view of Red Square and the Kremlin

Throughout the history of Moscow Red Square has been integral part of the Kremlin ensemble. Its original name was Poloye ("waste") place, or Pozhar ("fire"). Later it turned into the city's main market place known as Torg. In the 17th century it was given its present-day name of Red Square which means "beautiful" in Slavonic. The square has been the site of most

important events in Russian history. It witnessed long festive religious processions, royal trains and arrivals of foreign embassies. People crowded here to listen to the royal edicts that were proclaimed from Lobnoye Mesto ("place of a skull") – a circular platform faced with stone slabs. Lobnoye Mesto was also the site of public prayers and executions.

In 1612 the Russian army led by Kuzma Minin and Dmitry Pozharsky marched across Red Square to the Kremlin to drive the Poles out. To commemorate the event the monument to Minin and Pozharsky was set up here in 1818. In 1812 Napoleon inspected his troops on the square, yet soon suffered a crushing defeat. In 1945 after the end of World War II, the Victory Parade

was held on Red Square, with soldiers from all the fronts taking part in it.

Near the Kremlin wall, situated in the central axis of the square, is the Mausoleum, the shrine of Vladimir Lenin, founder of the Soviet State. It was built in 1930 by the famous architect Alexey Shchusev. The strict and precise forms of the structure tiled with marble, labradorite, granite and porphyry are in tune with the Kremlin ensemble. Behind the Mausoleum there is the cemetery of prominent Soviet statesmen and public figures, such as Iosif Stalin, Georgy Zhukov, Alexey Gorky and Yury Gagarin.

In its architectural perfection and beauty Red Square can rival the most famous squares in the world like Piazza di San Marco in Venice, square in front of St Peter's Cathedral in Rome and Place de la Concorde in Paris.

171

170. Spasskaya Tower of the Kremlin

171. Mausoleum of Vladimir Lenin.
Sarcophagus containing the body of Lenin

172. Red Square. Mausoleum of Vladimir Lenin. 1930.
Architect A. Shchusev
→
173. Red Square. View from Vasilyevsky Descent

172

174

Cathedral of St Basil the Blessed (Cathedral of the Intercession)

The cathedral was built by order of Ivan the Terrible and with the blessing of Metropolitan Macarius to commemorate an important event – the victory of the Russian army over the Kazan Khanate and final liberation of Russia from the Tartar-Mongol yoke, as a result of which the Russian lands were united with Moscow as their capital. The concept of a cathedral–monument brought forth the unusual architectural forms: nine churches are set on a lofty pedestal, eight of them are grouped round the central Church of the Intercession, whose hipped roof towers above the others at a height of 47.5 m. Its original colours had been more austere, it was only in the 17th – 18th centuries that the bright polychrome colouring of the domes and floral ornamentation of the lower tiers were introduced.

The cathedral is dedicated to the Intercession of the Mother of God as the city of Kazan was captured on that feast day, yet its other name is better known. In 1588 the popular "fool for Christ" Vasily, or Basil the Blessed, was buried

174. Red Square. Cathedral of the Intercession "on-the-Moat" (Cathedral of St Basil the Blessed). 1555–61. Architect Postnik Barma

175, 176. Red Square. Cathedral of St Basil the Blessed. Porch and detail of the hipped roof

in the north-east corner of the cathedral. Being the only one who dared to tell the truth to Ivan IV the Terrible, he was greatly revered by the people. A church dedicated to St Basil was added to the existing structure directly above his tomb, and since then the whole ensemble is commonly referred to as the Cathedral of St Basil the Blessed.

Located on the territory of the cathedral complex is the monument to Kuzma Minin and Dmitry Pozharsky transferred here after the construction of the Mausoleum of Vladimir Lenin in Red Square.

177. Red Square. Cathedral of St Basil the Blessed. Iconostasis

178. Red Square. Cathedral of St Basil the Blessed. Inner portal

179. Red Square. Monument to Kuzma Minin and Dmitry Pozharsky. 1804–18. Sculptor I. Martos

177

178

179

ГРАЖДАНИНУ МИНИНУ И КНЯЗЮ ПОЖАРСКОМУ
БЛАГОДАРНАЯ РОССІЯ. ЛѢТА 1818

182

183

184

180–182. View of the cupolas of the Cathedral of St Basil the Blessed

183. Red Square. Cathedral of the Intercession "on-the-Moat"
(Cathedral of St Basil the Blessed)

Next to the Cathedral of St Basil the Blessed there stand two buildings imitating 17th-century structures, though they were put up in the 19th century. These are the State Historical Museum and former Upper Trading Arcade, known nowadays as GUM. This enormous department store, with glass roofs of its passages, graceful bridges and fountains, houses not only shops but also cafes, restaurants and halls for fashion shows.

184. Red Square. Upper Trading Arcade (GUM). 1889–93. Architect A. Pomerantsev and engineer V. Shukhov

185. Red Square. GUM (State Department Store). Main hall

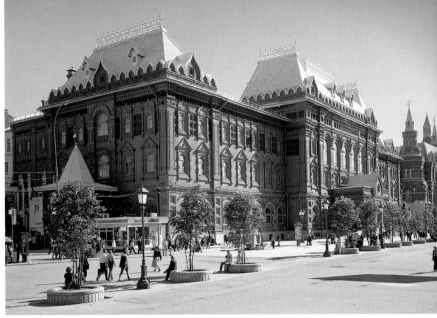

Manege Square

After the victory over Napoleon in 1812 and after the catastrophic retreat of the French troops Moscow was rapidly restored and rebuilt. In 1817 a new plan for the development of the ancient capital was introduced by the specially organized Construction Committee. It launched a great programme of rebuilding, which included a partial replanning of the city centre. The Russian architect Osip Bove played a big part in its work. In accordance with the 1817 plan a number of famous architectural ensembles appeared in Moscow and some improvements were made in the area round the Kremlin. The system of water basins and canals dating from the 18th century, when the Neglinnaya River bed had been reconstructed, was filled in and the Neglinnaya was diverted into a subterranian conduit. In 1821–23 Bove laid out the Alexander

←

186, 189. Manege Square. The State Historical Museum. 1874–83. Architects V. Shervud and A. Popov; engineer A. Semyonov
Monument to Marshal Georgy Zhukov. 1995. Sculptor V. Klykov and architect Yu. Grigoryev

187, 188. Manege Square. Building of the former City Duma (City Council). 1890–91. Architect D. Chichagov

190. View of the Iversky (Resurrection) Gate and the State Historical Museum

192

Gardens near the Kremlin wall where the Grotto and the Gate were erected soon after. In 1822 the architect F. Shestakov designed and built the fence around the Gardens.

At that time Manege Square was being formed. In 1817 the monumental edifice of Manege designed by Bove and Spanish engineer A. Betancourt was erected in the square, its architectural form being simple, yet imposing. The Manege's mighty Doric colonnade topped by the massive pediment without any sculptural decoration dominates the square. The unique wooden framework of its ceiling was considered a wonder of technology: the ceiling has a span of 45 m with no support in the middle. The Manege was intended for army drills and parades and its interior was so spacious that a whole regiment numbering about 2,000 soldiers could freely manoeuvre inside. Nowadays most representative Moscow, all-Russia and international shows are held here. Its exhibition area is 6,500 m².

In 1817–19 another Classical architect Domenico Gilliardi restored the building of Moscow University damaged in the war of 1812, which still stands in the square. Manege Square also features two largest hotels of the capital – the *National* built in the beginning of the 20th century and *Moscow* erected on Manege Square only in 1933–35. This high-rise building now dominates the place.

191. Panoramic view of Manege Square from the Kremlin

192. View of the Kremlin and Manege Square from the National *hotel*

→
193, 194. Manege Square. Central glass semicircular pavilion of the Okhotny Ryad *underground market*

In accordance with the new plan the Kitay-gorod territory was bounded with a semicircular chain of public squares starting up from the Moscow River and linked with the Kremlin esplanade by Theatre Square. It was then that the square assumed its present-day rectangular shape with one side slanted by the Kitay-gorod wall. To rebalance the irregularity a triangular garden was laid out by the wall. Located on the opposite side in the middle is the Bolshoi Theatre.

195. Alexander Garden. Eternal flame at the Tomb of the Unknown Soldier

196. Manege Square. The Iversky (Resurrection) Gate. Restored in 1995. Architect O. Zhurin

197. Alexander Garden. Guard of Honour at the Tomb of the Unknown Soldier

198. Fountain in Manege Square. 1990s. Sculptor Z. Tsereteli
→
199. Alexander Garden

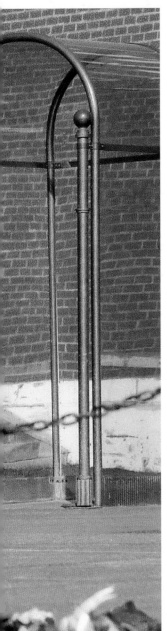

198

197

Bolshoi Theatre

In the middle of Theatre Square, opposite the garden, there stands the building of the Bolshoi (former Peter) Theatre. It has an imposing portico supported by eight columns and topped with the bronze sculpture of Apollo's chariot. The portico forms the main axis of the square ensemble. It was constructed in 1856 by A. Kavos on the site of the magnificent structure designed by O. Bove that had been destroyed by fire some time before. The building of the Bolshoi Theatre is one of the best examples of Russian architecture

202

from the mid-19th century and a largest theatre structure in Europe. It is the leading opera house of the country and one of the most popular opera and ballet companies in Europe. Staged here have been operas by Mikhail Glinka, Alexander Dargomyzhsky, Modest Moussorgsky, Alexander Borodin, Nikolay Rimsky-Korsakov and operas and

200. Bolshoi Theatre. Ceiling painting. Restored in 1955 by a group of artists led by P. Korin

201. Bolshoi Theatre. 1821–24. Architects O. Bove and A. Mikhailov; 1855–56. Architect A. Kavos

202. Colonnade of the Bolshoi Theatre. Detail

201

203. Bolshoi Theatre. Auditorium

204. Bolshoi Theatre. Scene from Prince Igor
opera by Alexander Borodin

205. Bolshoi Theatre. Scene from The Sleeping
Beauty *ballet by Pyotr Tchaikovsky*
→

206. Bolshoi Theatre

ballets by Pyotr Tchaikovsky. The theatre has been famous for its brilliant singers, dancers, conductors and stage-set artists. Such names as Fyodor Chaliapin, Leonid Sobinov, Antonina Nezhdanova, Yekaterina Geltser, Sergey Rakhmaninov and Konstantin Korovin are the pride of both Russian and world culture. The famous Russian singers Ivan Kozlovsky, Sergey Lemeshev, Nadezhda Obukhova and ballet dancers Marina Semenova, Galina Ulanova and Asaf Messerer performed here. Among the company's best productions are operas *Boris Godunov, Khovanshchina, Sadko, War and Peace, Othello, Aida, Don Carlos* and ballets *Swan Lake, Nutcracker, Romeo and Juliet, Spartak* and many others.

207

208

Maly Theatre
Metropol Hotel

The square has got its name by no chance. Besides the Bolshoi Theatre there is also the Maly Theatre, the house of the oldest Russian drama company, with the monument to Alexander Ostrovsky standing in front of it. The Maly Theatre is often called "Ostrovsky's house," as 50 plays by this famous 19th-century Russian playwright have been staged here.

Another highlight of the square is the *Metropol* hotel designed in the early 20th century in the Art Nouveau style. Its plain facades are rather impressive. The ground floor is made of red granite and the upper floors are crowned with a big sculptured frieze and a ceramic panel *Princess Reverie* by Mikhail Vrubel. The sophisticated silhouette of the top part forms the smooth line of the roof against the blue sky.

207. View of the Maly Theatre. 1824. Architect O. Bove; 1842. Architect K. Thon

208. Maly Theatre. Auditorium

209. Apollo's chariot atop the Bolshoi Theatre building. 1856. Sculptor P. Klodt

210. Metropol hotel. 1899–1903. Architect V. Walcott

Tverskaya Street

Tverskaya (in the Soviet period Gorky) Street is the main street of Moscow. Known since the 14th century it became the city's major thoroughfare in the 15th – 17th centuries when relations with north-western Russian principalities, primarily Tver and Novgorod, began to play an important part in Moscow's economy. Another impact was given to its development
in the 18th century when the new capital of St Petersburg was founded in the north. It was Tverskaya Street that all who came to Moscow from St Petersburg and vice versa travelled along. Though greatly changed, the street retained its representative

211

212

211. Tverskaya Square.
Office of the Moscow Government

212. Tverskaya Street

213. Monument to Prince Yury Dolgoruky. 1954.
Sculptors S. Orlov, A. Antropov and N. Shtamm;
architect V. Andreyev

РАДИО ТЕЛЕФОН

character. It was wider and busier and looked more ceremonial than other streets. In accordance with the Soviet plan for Moscow's reconstruction Gorky Street was the first to undergo certain improvements. Some of its buildings were demolished, others moved to other sites as a result of which the street became 2.5 times wider, thus the architects emphasized its leading role among other streets.

Tverskaya Street links several squares. Pushkin (former Strastnaya) Square, though much altered, better than others answers its original purpose of public square. The history of another square is no less complicated. It came into existence

214. *Panoramic view of Tverskaya Street at night*

215. *Central Telegraph Office in Tverskaya Street*

216. *Rozhdestvenka. Savoy hotel*

217. *Tverskaya Street. Former Yeliseyevs' food shop. Sales area*

218. *Tverskaya Street. Former Filippov's bakery*

219. *Tverskaya Street. Former Yeliseyevs' food shop*

218

217

219

in the late 18th century when it was designed by M. Kazakov as a drill ground in front of the Moscow Governor-General house. In the second half of the 1930s it was widened and built with multi-storeyed houses, thus assuming more austere and ceremonial character to match the style of the Moscow City Council Office (where the city authorities sit now) that stands in it.

220. Pushkin Square

221. Tverskaya Street, a major thoroughfare of the city

222. Pushkin Square. Monument to Alexander Pushkin. 1880. Sculptor A. Opekushin

State Pushkin Museum
of Fine Arts

223. State Pushkin Museum of Fine Arts.
1898–1912. Architect R. Klein,
sculptor G. Zaleman

224. Main staircase of the museum

225. State Pushkin Museum of Fine Arts.
Italian courtyard: one of the museum rooms

The world-famous Museum of Fine Arts is a major centre for the study of Western European art in Russia, second only in importance and scope to the renowned Hermitage in St Petersburg. The idea of creating a collection within the fine art and antiquities department of Moscow University which would cover all periods in the development of world art history and above all act as an educational insti-

tution received public approval in the mid-19th century. Philologist, art historian and Moscow University professor Ivan Tsvetayev was charged with formulating the aims of the project, devising a programme and organizing all planning and building work. The building assumed the form of a Greek temple on a high podium, with a Ionic colonnade at the central facade. The first-floor rooms have

226

227

228

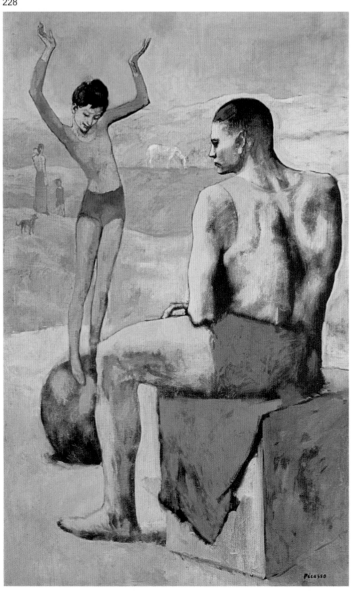

229

glass ceilings designed by the well-known engineers I. Rerberg and V. Shukhov. The Alexander III Museum of Fine Arts affiliated to Moscow University was opened on May 31, 1912. In the 1920s and 1930s its holdings increased considerably after the nationalization of private art collections, reorganization of the Moscow Public and Rumyantsev Museums, the addition of collections from the country estates outside Moscow and the closure of the Ostroukhov

226. *Giovanni Antonio Boltraffio. C. 1467–1516*
St Sebastian. *C. 1500*

227. *Rembrandt. 1606–1669*
Ahasuerus, Haman and Esther. *1660*

228. *Pablo Picasso. 1881–1973*
Girl on a Ball. *1905*

229. *Pierre-Auguste Renoir. 1841–1919*
Girls in Black. *Early 1880s*

230. *Henri Matisse. 1869–1954*
Still Life with Goldfish. *1911*

231. *Edgar Degas. 1834–1917*
Blue Dancers. *C. 1898*

232. *Henri Rousseau. 1844–1910*
Jaguar Attacking a Horse. *1910*

Museum of Painting and Icon-painting.
Later, in the 1940s, the museum received
unique exhibits from the former Museum
of New Western Art (the collections of
S. Shchukin and I. Morozov). After receiv-
ing these private collections as well as
works by Old Masters from the Hermitage
the Museum of Fine Arts gained considerable
status among the major world museums.
At present its holdings number more than
a million original paintings and graphic
works, and even more sculptures and
objects of applied art from all over the
world, from antiquity to the present day.

233. Lucas Cranach. 1472–1553
Virgin and the Child

234. Claude Gellee, called Lorrain. 1600–1682
The Rape of Europa. *1655*

235. Paul Gauguin. 1848–1903
Are You Jealous? *1892*

234

235

Cathedral
of Christ the Saviour

←

*236. Cathedral of Christ the Saviour. Architect K. Thon.
Restored in the 1990s*

237. Cupola of the bell chapel of the Transfiguration Church

*238. View of the Cathedral of Christ the Saviour and monument
to Alexander II from Lenivka Street*

The Cathedral of Christ the Saviour is situated in the city centre,
not far from the Kremlin, on the high bank of the Moscow River,
the Kropotkin Embankment.

In the Middle Ages the territory belonged to the St Alexius Nunnery. Later it was transferred to another place. According to tradition, its abbess ordered to be chained to the nunnery wall and
foretold that everything constructed here would be later destroyed.
Nevertheless, it was on the place that it was decided to build a
cathedral commemorating a most important event in Russian history – the victory over Napoleon in the Patriotic War, which was
to be in accord with the composition of the nearby Kremlin.

240

239. Lower circuit gallery
(Gallery of Military Glory)

240. Central and altar parts of the Cathedral
of Christ the Saviour
→
241. View of the main iconostasis

The architect of the project Konstantin Thon was the founder and leader of the so-called Russo-Byzantine style, an official church style of the mid-19th century. He succeeded in his design in giving most comprehensive expression to the ideological programme of the government whose essence was formulated by emperor Nicholas I in the motto "Orthodoxy, Autocracy and Nationality". Besides the Cathedral of Christ the Saviour, Thon was famous as the architect of the Grand Kremlin Palace and State Armoury.

242. Main iconostasis. North-east part. Detail

243. Main iconostasis. Central part. Detail

244. Main iconostasis. South-east part. Detail

244

The appearance of this imposing architectural ensemble seriously changed the view of the Kremlin, its river facade began to look more monumental, representative and majestic.

In 1830 Thon took part, with other Russian architects, in the competition for the best design of the Cathedral of Christ the Saviour. In 1832 Nicholas I approved Thon's design because in his project the new cathedral was in tune with the Kremlin architecture. It was modelled on the Kremlin cathedrals of the Dormition and Archangel Michael.

246

Its size was enormous. It was 103 m high, its area was 6,805 m^2 and the central dome's diameter 25.5 m. Construction of the grandiose edifice which could accommodate 10,000 people went on for dozens of years. Thousands of people took part in it. These were architects, technical workers and masons, the whole process was supervised by Thon himself. The foundation was laid in 1839 and only in 1881 the idea of the architect was completely realized. Thon died in the beginning of the same year, so the Cathedral of Christ

245. Enthronization of His Holiness Patriarch Cyril. 1 February 2009

246. Ceremonial Easter service

247. Painting in the main sanctuary: Last Supper and the "High Place" (from the first Cathedral)

the Saviour is justifiably considered the main creation in the prominent architect's career. The consecration of the cathedral took place in 1889 after which daily services began there.

The white-stone magnificent structure is crowned, like the Dormition Cathedral of the Kremlin, with five gilded cupolas. Beautiful staircases lead to the church. The marble belt with basreliefs showing scenes from the Bible and Holy History ran along the facades above the portals. The cathedral was lavishly ornamented. Outstanding sculptors (P. Klodt, A. Loganovsky, N. Ramazanov and F. Tolstoy) were invited to decorate it. The murals inside were painted by famous Russian artists (F. Bruni, T. Neff, I. Surikov, V. Vereshchagin, G. Semiradsky and others).

In 1931 the cathedral was exploded. An enormous House of the Soviets was began to be constructed here. But when World War II started, its metallic framework was melted. In 1960 the *Moscow* swimming pool was built on the foundation. On the 7th of January 1994, the Moscow government decided to restore the Cathedral of Christ the Saviour. Nowadays

248. The Fatherland painting on the main dome ceiling

249. Child Jesus Christ Surrounded by Angels painting on the south cupola ceiling

251

252

254

←
250. East facade of the Cathedral of Christ the Saviour

←
251. South facade of the Cathedral of Christ the Saviour. High relief: David Returning in Triumph After His Victory over Goliath

←
252. Cathedral of Christ the Saviour. South facade. Larger middle door

253. View of the Cathedral of Christ the Saviour from St Nicholas' Church "at Bersenevo"

254. Chapel in front of the Cathedral of Christ the Saviour

255. Holy Trinity Church "at Bersenevo" (with side-altar dedicated to St Nicholas). 1656–57

the cathedral, a most important sacred place of the Russian Orthodox Church and symbol of the unification of the nation, stands on its historical place. People from all parts of the country have donated money for its restoration. It looks exactly like the original structure, though the latest methods and materials have been applied. In the January of 2000 it was consecrated and opened for daily services. The square in front of the cathedral is used for concerts of choirs. There is an observation platform in the upper part of the cathedral. There is a church museum here, its exhibits and films tell about the construction, destruction and restoration of the cathedral.

255

Zamoskvorechye is the oldest and, probably, best preserved district in the city's centre. It is distinguished by the peculiar planning of its main streets – Bolshaya Polyanka, Bolshaya Ordynka and Pyatnitskaya. They are lined with mansions of merchants in the styles of Neoclassicism (for example, those of A. Dolgov, N. Kireyevskaya and A. Arsenyeva in Bolshaya Ordynka), Historicism (such as the mansions of M. Reck and T. Korobkov in Pyatnitskaya and the house of N. Igumnov in Bolshaya Yakimanka) and Art Nouveau (mansion of I. Petrov in Bolshaya Ordynka) as well as apartment houses for rent built in the late 19th – early 20th centuries and numerous Christian Orthodox churches. Most noteworthy of Zamoskvorechye religious structures are the churches of St Nicholas "at Pyzhi" (1670s), St Catherine (1766–75), the Icon of the Mother of God "The Joy of All Who Sorrow" (1783–91; 1828–36) in Bolshaya Ordynka, St Clement, Bishop of Rome (1756–70), the Holy Trinity "at Vishnyaki" (1804–11) in Pyatnitskaya, St Gregory the Wonderworker of Neo-Caesarea (1662–79) in Bolshaya Polyanka and St John the Soldier (1709–17) in Yakimanka.

The Sophiyskaya Embankment is the front line of Zamoskvorechye. It encircles the island formed in 1783–86 after the construction of the Drainage Canal. The old buildings in the Sophiyskaya Embankment are among most interesting in Moscow's architecture. The expressive silhouettes of the hipped roof of the tall bell tower (1868) of St Sophia's Church in Sredniye Sadovniki put up in 1682–85 on the site of a 15th-century wooden church and the imposing dome of the former House of Free Apartments owned by the Bakhrushin brothers (1900–03) echo the Moscow Kremlin structures. Of note are also the house of merchant Lobkov in the Empire style (*c.* 1816; 1914) and the former mansion of I. Kharitonenko, now the residence of the English ambassador (1891–93) in the Art Nouveau style.

256. View of the Sophiyskaya Embankment and the district of Zamoskvorechye

State Tretyakov Gallery

The Tretyakov Gallery is one of the most famous art museums in the world. Its collection covers a whole millennium of Russian cultural development.

The founder was a Moscow merchant and industrialist who was also a great art expert, connoisseur and renowned patron: Pavel Tretyakov. In 1860 he wrote in his bequest: "I would like to form a national gallery collection comprising only paintings by Russian artists," which he devoted his entire life to. Every year he added what he considered to be the finest works of art to the gallery, buying paintings directly from the artists, their studios or exhibitions. Tretyakov's interests were wideranging. His collection presented Russian art in all its variety and historical development. It included not only pictures by contemporary artists but also works from the 18th – 19th centuries, as well

259

260

257. Andrey Rublev. C. 1360/1370 – 1430s.
Icon of the Holy Trinity. 1410s

258. State Tretyakov Gallery. 1901–03.
Facade designed by Victor Vasnetsov

259. State Tretyakov Gallery.
Exhibition of Early Russian Art

260. State Tretyakov Gallery.
Main staircase

261. St George and the Dragon.
First quarter of the 16th century.
Central Russia

261

262

as specimens of early Russian icon-painting. Originally they were displayed in the mansion of the Tretyakovs in Lavrushinsky Lane, the district of Zamoskvorechye. The collection had greatly expanded by the 1870s and for the following twenty years the owners had to build several new structures for its exhibitions. The famous colourful facade uniting the entire complex of buildings was erected after the death of Tretyakov between 1901 and 1903, to a design by the eminent Russian artist Victor Vasnetsov. This Russian-style structure is a symbol of national art.

The already-famous gallery was opened to public view in 1881, during Tretyakov's lifetime. In 1892, just a few years before his death, Tretyakov donated his superb collection to the city of Moscow, then it numbered 1,287 paintings, 518 drawings and 9 sculptures by 18th- and 19th-century masters.

262. Karl Briullov. 1799–1852
Rider. *1832*

263. Ivan Shishkin. 1832–1898
Morning in a Pine Forest. *1889*

264. Victor Vasnetsov. 1848–1926
Bogatyrs (Warriors). *1898*

265. Vasily Perov. 1834–1882
Hunters Resting. *1871*

263

264

265

266

267

268

269

270

266. *Pavel Fedotov. 1815–1852*
A Major's Marriage Proposal. *1848*

267. *State Tretyakov Gallery.*
Surikov Room

268. *Vasily Surikov. 1848–1916*
Boyarynia Morozova. *1887*

269. *Isaac Levitan. 1860–1900*
Golden Autumn. *1895*

270. *Alexey Savrasov. 1830–1897*
Rooks Have Returned. *1871*

271

272

273

274

After the death of Tretyakov the gallery kept growing. In the 1920s it absorbed some nationalized collections of the richest Moscow art patrons and connoisseurs. The department of 20th-century art was organized in the 1920s. It boasts many masterpieces by best Russian avant-garde painters.

In the mid-1970s the gallery was donated one of the richest art collections in the world amassed by Georgy Kostaki. Today the Tretyakov Gallery collection consists of more than 100,000 works of art displayed at the department of early Russian art from the 12th to 17th centuries, the department of painting, graphics and sculpture from the 18th to early 20th centuries and the department of 20th-century art. Part of its stocks is on view in another building located on Krymsky Val.

Monasteries, Cathedrals and Churches

Moscow, the religious centre of Russia, is famous for its churches. A rare example of the combination of church and secular architecture from the 17th – 19th centuries is to be found in the Bersenevskaya Embankment, opposite the Cathedral of Christ the Saviour. This is the ensemble

276. Monastery of the Don Icon of the Mother of God. Founded in 1591
Bell tower above the west gate. 1730–32.
Architect Domenico Trezzini; 1742–55.
Architects A. Yevlashev and D. Ukhtomsky

277. House of deacon Abercius Kirillov.
1657; 1703–11

278. Church of the Intercession at Fili.
View of the iconostasis

279. Church of the Intercession at Fili. 1693

276

278

277

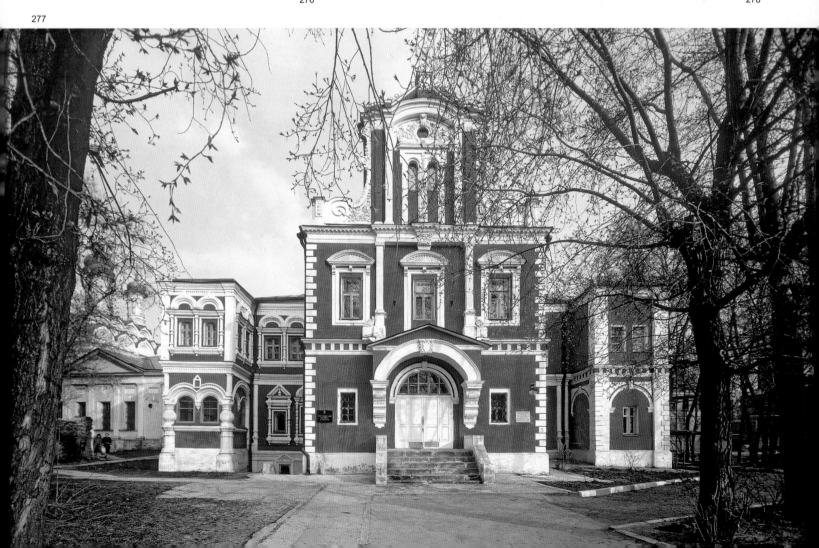

of the former estate of Abercius Kirillov (1622–1682), the chief gardener of Tsar Alexey Mikhailovich, since 1677 the Duma deacon who headed the Treasury and Parish ministries. The white-stone house was erected in 1657 on the foundation of 15th- and 16th-century buildings. In 1703–11 the front facade with an attic storey in the "Dutch" taste of Peter the Great was added to the house. Next to it stands the magnificent five-domed Church of St Nicholas "at Bersenevo" (1656–57), its composition is similar to that of St George's Church "at Yendovo" (1653). It is notable for its refined sculptural decor and picturesque tiles of the north entrance and porch (1690s).

In one of the oldest parts of Moscow, Khamovniky, a few ancient buildings including the Church of St Nicholas have survived.

In the 17th century there used to be water meadows owned by the grand prince. Soon *khamovniki*, court weavers, were settled here, hence the name of the district. They built the Church of St Nicholas and decorated it with three tiers of *kokoshniks* (semicircular false gables) and bright multi-coloured tiles.

The Church of the Intercession at Fili was built by an unknown architect on the ancestral estate of the boyar Lev Naryshkin, uncle of Peter the Great, the church is a striking example of the Moscow Baroque style. Rich decoration of the interior creates an impression of radiance, festivity and lavish splendour.

280. Monastery of the Meeting of Our Lord. Founded in 1397

281. Church of the Krutitsk Metropolitan. 16th – 17th century. Architect O. Startsev

282. Church of the Resurrection at Kadashi. 1687–95

283. Novospassky (New Saviour) Monastery. Founded in the 14th century

281

282

283

284. *Church of St Nicholas at Khamovniki. 1679–82*

285. *Church of the Ascension of Our Lord (Large Ascension Church) near the Nikitsky Gate. 1820s*

286. *Church of the Conception by St Anna of the Mother of God. Late 16th century*

287. *Monastery of the Don Icon of the Mother of God. The Large Cathedral of the Don Icon of the Mother of God. 1684–98*

285

286

The white walls of one of the oldest Moscow monasteries stand on the high bank of the Yauza, the second largest river in Moscow, at the mouth of the Zolotoy Rozhok tributary. The St Andronicus Monastery of the Saviour was founded in the mid-14th century by Metropolitan Alexius,

287

288

to commemorate his miraculous deliverance from death.
The monastery was named after its first abbot St Andronicus. The monastery is most famous as the place where the
great monk and icon-painter Andrey Rublev led his ascetic
life. Rublev died here and was buried beside the cathedral.

288. Church of the Theophany at Yelokhovo. 1837–45. Architect E. Tiurin

289. St Andronicus Monastery of the Saviour. Icon of St George. Early 16th century

290. Church at Bolshye Viazemy. 1597–99

291. Church of St John the Soldier at Yakimanka. 1709–13

292. St Andronicus Monastery of the Saviour. Cathedral of the Saviour. 1410–27

204

289

290

291

292

Novodevichy Convent

293. Novodevichy Convent. Founded in 1524

Numerous fires devastated Moscow in the past when most of its buildings were wooden. The 14th-century chronicle mentions "six great fires" which burnt the city to ashes. Moscow was also greatly damaged by foreign invaders. That's why very few samples of ancient architecture are preserved now. But the less they are in number, the more we value them as unique creations of Russian genius. Most of the churches were stone so they could withstand both fires and invaders.

The Novodevichy Convent, one of the most beautiful monastic ensembles in Russia,

has been a branch of the State Historical
Museum since 1934. It was founded by
order of Prince Vasily III in 1524, to commemorate the 1514 victory of Russia over
the Polish and Lithuanian forces in the
battle for the borderlands and the return
of the town of Smolensk. Situated near
the road leading to Moscow from the
south, it served as a military outpost on
more than one occasion. The convent was
favoured by the tsars and boyars, since the
nuns included members of both royal and
high-ranking families. Among them was
notorious princess Sophia who organized

294

a rebellion against her half brother Peter I. The architectural ensemble was formed from the 16th to 17th centuries. The ancient convent cathedral was dedicated to the Smolensk icon of the Mother of God coming from Byzantium. It was a mostly revered icon in the Smolensk Province.

294. Panoramic view of the Novodevichy Convent from the pond

295. View of the Tsaritsyna Tower (17th century). Lopukhin Chambers and the gateway Transfiguration Church (1687–88)

296. Novodevichy Convent. Cathedral of the Smolensk Icon of the Mother of God (1524–25). Architect Alovisio Novo (?)

297. Novodevichy Convent. Church of the Dormition of the Mother of God with refectory (1685–87)

295

296

297

←
*298. Smolensk Icon of the Mother of God.
16th century. From the Local Saints tier
in the iconostasis of the Cathedral of the
Smolensk Icon of the Mother of God*
←
*299. Cathedral of the Smolensk Icon
of the Mother of God. View of the
iconostasis*

*300, 301. Cathedral of the Smolensk Icon
of the Mother of God. Iconostasis*

*302. Cathedral of the Smolensk Icon
of the Mother of God*

Kolomenskoye

The State Historical, Architectural and Landscape Museum of Kolomenskoye is located in the south of Moscow. Kolomenskoye was particularly important during the reign of Ivan the Terrible in the 16th century and Alexey Mikhailovich in the 17th century. The unique architectural ensemble was built at the period.

The dominant structure at Kolomenskoye is the Church of the Ascension. In the 16th century it served as a summer church for the tsar's family. It was erected

to mark a momentous event – the birth of
a long-awaited heir to the Russian throne,
the future Ivan IV, called Ivan the Terrible.
The church reaches a height of 62 m.
In 1667–71 a festive-looking palace decorated with fanciful wood carvings was
erected in Kolomenskoye. It was, however,
dismantled in the 18th century.

Today the Museum-Preserve of Kolomenskoye is well known for its folk festivals.

303. *Panoramic view of Kolomenskoye*

304. *Kolomenskoye. Church of the Kazan Icon
of the Mother of God. 1649–50*

305. *Festival of folk music in Kolomenskoye*

306. *Kolomenskoye. Church of the Ascension. 1532*

Estates and Mansions

Extant in present-day Moscow are a number of dwelling houses built after the fire of 1812. These include not only some unique architectural structures but also standardized buildings made after specially designed models. When we look at them we can imagine a quiet and old-fashioned life lived by the owners of these houses that once were scattered all over Moscow. Bove, Gilliardi and Grigoryev were among the best-known architects of the period dwelling houses and mansions.

At the end of the 19th century many-storeyed apartment houses for rent

307. Peter Palace (Peter Castle). 1776–96. Architect M. Kazakov

308, 312. Estate of the Usachevs (Naydenovs). 1829–31. Architect D. Gilliardi; 1836. Architect A. Grigoryev (?)

309. Mansion of V. Gribov. 1909. Architects A. Miliukov and B. Velikovsky

310. Wing of I. Rimsky-Korsakov's estate. 1840s

311. House of A. Polivanov. 1822–23

307

308

310

309

311

312

appeared in Moscow. One of these is the house of P. Pertsov. This typical Art Nouveau edifice is one of the most impressive and festive-looking in Moscow. Especially noteworthy are the complex configuration of the house, its steeply-pitched roof, ceramic representations of the sun, mermaids, exotic animals and plants.

*313. Mansion of Riabushinsky. 1900.
Architect F. Shekhtel*

314. Mansion of Riabushinsky. Main staircase

*315. House-Museum of Chaliapin.
Building of the 18th century*

*316. Building of the former Loan Bank. 1913–16.
Architects V. Pokrovsky and B. Nilus*

*317. Nikolskaya Street. Building of the former
Synod printing house. 1814. Architect I. Mironovsky*

318. In a side-street of Old (Stary) Arbat

313

314

315

316

317

318

319

320

The building of the Loan Bank is designed in the Neo-Russian style. Its central facade combining the representative character of modern public institution with the elegance of 17th-century palace is most impressive.

Among the most interesting historical and architectural monuments of great artistic value on Nikolskaya Street is the Royal Printing House, which played an important role in the advance of learning in this country.

319. Former apartment house of P. Pertsov. 1906–10. Architect N. Zhukov, after the drawings of the artist S. Maliutin

320. House of A. Demidov. 1770s. Restored in 1814. Iron fence cast in the 1780s after the drawings of the artist F. Argunov

321. Mansion of V. Gribov. Sculpture at the main entrance

322. Palace of K. Razumovsky (former English Club). 1780. Restored after 1812. Architect Adam Menelas

323. Rozhdestvensky Boulevard

321

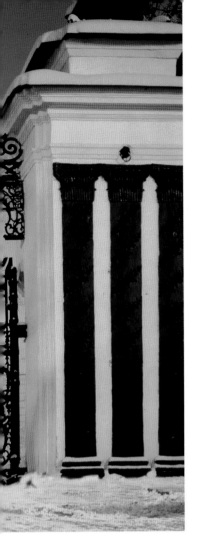

322

324

Kuskovo

Kuskovo is first mentioned as the country estate of boyar V. Sheremetyev at the beginning of the 16th century. The famous palace ensemble and park appeared in the second half of the 18th century. Count Pyotr Sheremetyev, an important member of the nobility at the Russian Imperial Court, state functionary and collector of art and antiquities was its first owner. The palace was constructed in the style of early Neoclassicism by serf craftsmen. Its austere exterior and luxurious interiors demonstrated the refined taste of the owner.

Kuskovo is the oldest park on the outskirts of Moscow, although what remains is only part of the sweeping expanse that was once the pride of the Sheremetyevs. The regular French-style park was laid out in the 1750s – 1760s and featured pavilions, a conservatory and a collection of marble sculpture. Kuskovo was visited by Catherine the Great on several occasions. Up to 25,000 guests would flock here to lavish celebrations. The count decreed that the park should be open to the public in the summer months. In 1932 the Porcelain Museum was transferred here. Today it has a unique collection of ceramics produced by Russian and foreign factories from the 15th to 20th centuries and numbering 18,000 items.

324. Kuskovo. Palace. Second entrance hall

325. Kuskovo. Palace. 1769–75.
Architect K. Blank and others

326. Kuskovo. Grotto Pavilion. 1756–75.
Architect F. Argunov

327. Kuskovo. Dutch Pavilion. 1749

326

Ostankino

The Ostankino Theatre-Palace became famous worldwide two centuries ago. Like Kuskovo, it was a property of Nikolay Sheremetyev, the grandson of Boris Sheremetyev, Peter I's close associate, the first Russian count, a nobleman, leading statesman and collector of art and antiquities. The theatre was his main passion. Sheremetyev was famous for his celebrations, festivities and theatre performances that greatly impressed his contemporaries by their luxury and refined taste. The idea of creating a temple to Apollo was realized by Sheremetyev at Ostankino where he constructed his celebrated theatre.

328

The theatre had intricate machinery which produced special effects and the stage and auditorium could be transformed into a ballroom. A troupe of trained serf actors performed the best operas by both Western European and Russian composers. There were some 100 operas in their repertoire. The lovely Praskovya Kovalyova-Zhemchugova, darling of the public, performed with the company and became the wife of Count Sheremetyev in defiance of social convention.

The Ostankino palace was filled with family collections of paintings, sculpture, antique firearms and porcelain. The picture gallery once exhibited paintings by Titian, Rubens and Van Dyck but it was looted by Napoleon's soldiers in 1812. The Ostankino park employed both the English and French systems of landscape gardening, and was renowned for a rare collection of exotic foreign plants.

328. Ostankino. Palace. 1792–98. Architects F. Camporesi, A. Mironov, P. Argunov and others

329. Ostankino. Palace. Theatre. View of the auditorium

330. Ostankino. Palace. West suite of rooms on the ground floor

331. Panoramic view of the Moscow River.
Bolshoi (Large) Moskvoretsky Bridge

332. View of the Kremlin and the Bolshoi
(Large) Kamenny Bridge

→
333. Panoramic view of the Kremlin Embankment

Moscow High-Rise Buildings

From the second half of the 1930s to 1950s a great number of buildings that can boast perfect artistic quality were constructed in Moscow. The architectural trend once labelled as "excessive embellishment" is no longer condemned. It is considered to be the Neoclassical style now. At that time the architects were eager to create ensembles that would be in harmony with their elevated, triumphant mood and represent the ideals of the epoch. They were deliberate in using sumptuous, imposing forms. Such ensembles appeared in Tverskaya (former Gorky) Street and part of Kutuzovsky Prospect reconstructed before the mid-1950s. Most important architectural

complexes to be created all over Moscow at the period were the standardized high-rise buildings erected in commemoration of the 800th anniversary of Moscow and metro stations put up in the same period. These structures were perceived as the components of the one grandiose plan and added some new features to Moscow's outline, creating new vertical lines round which many districts' compositions were grouped.

The decision to construct high-rise buildings was made in 1947. They were to be located in most important and famous parts of Moscow and to mark the borders of the city's historical "nucleus."

334. Ukraine hotel. 1956.
Architects A. Mordvinov, V. Oltarzhevsky and V. Kalish

335. Panoramic view of the Moscow River

337

338

Thus, the building on the Kotelnicheskaya Embankment and the *Ukraine* hotel accentuated an important area along the Moscow River, the *Leningradskaya* hotel in Komsomolskaya Square indicated the most significant railway junction. Buildings on Smolenskaya, Kudrinskaya and Lermontovskaya squares singled out the intersections of major city thoroughfares in Sadovoye Ring. In their style all these

336. High-rise building in Kudrinskaya Square. 1950–54. Architects M. Posokhin and A. Mndoyants

337. High-rise building on the Kotelnicheskaya Embankment. 1949–53. Architects D. Chechulin and A. Fostkovsky

338. In Sadovoye Ring

339. View of Moscow taken from the Office of the Ministry of Foreign Affairs

339

340

340. Panoramic view of Smolenskaya Square

structures are representative of the so-called Stalin Neoclassicism of the 1930s. Their symmetrically organized facades are decorated with heavy moulding including many Soviet symbols.

The high-rise Office of the Ministry of Foreign Affairs in Smolenskaya Square is distinguished by a simple decor and the unity of composition. Its projecting pilasters contribute

to the monumentality of the structure. According to the original design, the building was to be crowned with a right-angled tower but Stalin himself changed the project and the building was topped with a tent-shaped spire.

The tallest structure of all the skyscrapers is the building on the Kotelnicheskaya Embankment. Located at the confluence

of the Moscow and Yauza rivers, it serves as a dominant feature and starting point of all the streets leading to the river and the Kremlin. 176 m high, it displays a heavy decor composed of statues and battlements. Like other structures of the kind, it is used by weather watch services.

The *Ukraine* hotel is situated at a curve of the Moscow River where it is intersected by New Arbat, one of Moscow's main streets, that leads into Kutuzovsky Prospect farther on. Together with the skyscraper on the Kotelnicheskaya Embankment it marks an important area along the Moscow River. The classical pyramidal obelisks atop its tiers alternate with the decorative attics made of five-pointed

341. Panoramic view of Moscow taken from the high-rise building on the Kotelnicheskaya Embankment

342. Dwelling house for the Central Executive Committee and Council of People's Commissars staff on the Bersenevskaya Embankment (known as the "House on the embankment"). 1928–31. Architects B. and D. Iofann

343. High-rise building near Krasnye Vorota. 1949–53. Architects A. Dushkin and B. Mesentsev
→
344. View of the Bersenevskaya Embankment from the Cathedral of Christ the Saviour

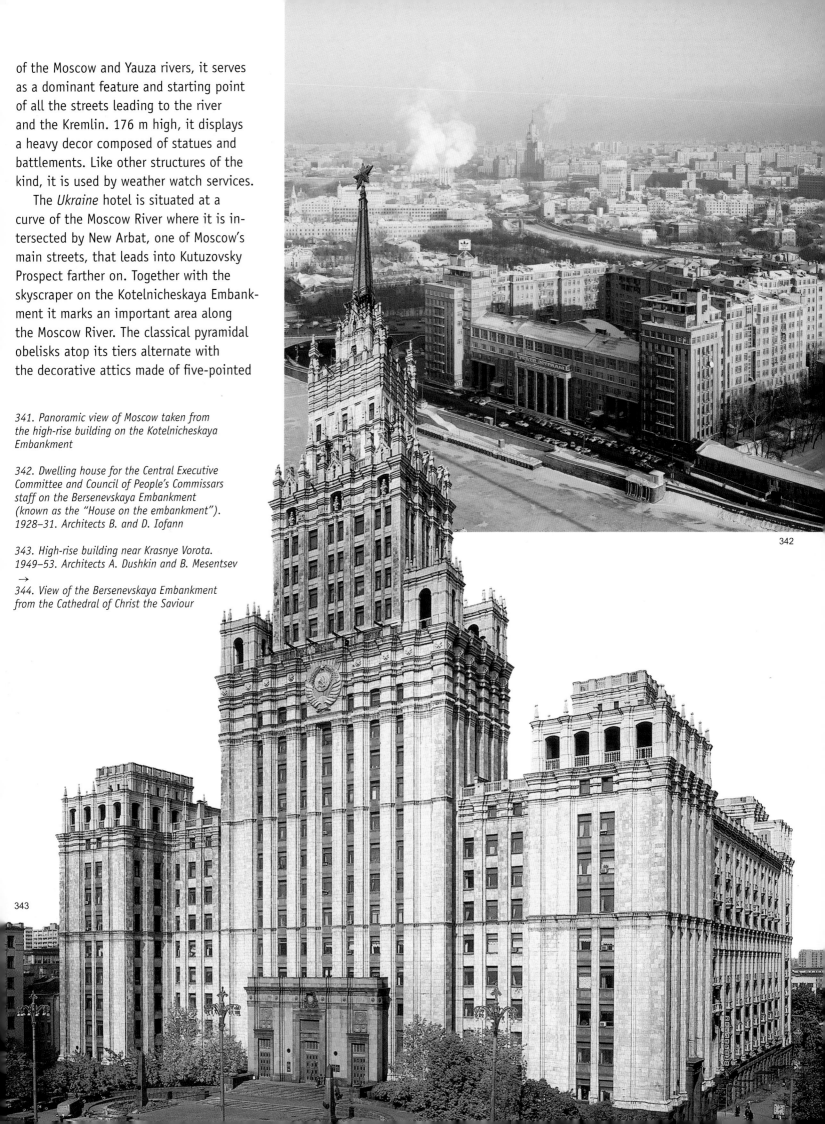

342

343

345

345. Moscow Zoo

→

346, 347. Main building of Moscow State University on Vorobyovy Hills. 1949–53. Architects L. Rudnev, S. Chernyshev, P. Abrosimov and A. Khryakov

stars and vases shaped as wheat sheaves. The structure is characterized by the balanced composition of its parts and accurate proportions. The hotel has 1,032 rooms. Many elements of the original furnishing have been preserved in its interiors, such as furniture, lamps, panel doors and ceiling mouldings.

The main building of Moscow State University was designed by the architects L. Rudnev, S. Chernyshev, P. Abrosimov and A. Khryakov and constructed on Vorobyovy Hills in 1949–53. It is the tallest and largest of all the high-rising structures erected in the first decade after World War II, its height being 238 m, including the spire, and its inner volume 1,335 m^3. Its artistic decoration as well as the decoration of the surrounding area was done by the sculptors and artists M. Anikushin, E. Vuchetich, S. Gerasimov, L. Kerbel, S. Konenkov, P. Korin, M. Manizer, G. Motovilov, V. Mukhina, G. Nissky, S. Orlov, A. Plastov, Ya. Romas, N. Tomsky and others.

All-Russia Exhibition Complex

The present-day All-Russia Exhibition Complex (named so since 1992) has been created on the basis of the former Exhibition of National Economic Achievements (VDNKh) (1939–41; 1954–58) and the All-Union Agricultural Exhibition. It is the largest public complex in Moscow, comparable in its size only to Moscow State University on Vorobyovy Hills. It has an area of 234 hectares and comprises 300 houses and 80 pavilions. Its original design was done in 1937 by V. Oltarzhevsky who took into consideration the planning of the First All-Russia Exhibition of Agriculture, Industry and Crafts organized in 1923. After the expansion of its territory and the construction of the new main entrance (architects L. Polyakov and I. Melchakov, sculptor G. Motovilov) the project was altered by A. Zhukov and R. Klix in 1954. The well-known monument by V. Mukhina, once expressing the Soviet ideal, the *Worker and Collective-farm Woman*, was set up at the main entrance in 1939. It had been made for the Soviet pavilion at the International Exhibition in Paris in 1937.

The main features organizing the architectural composition are two pavilions built in 1954: Central (97 m high, including the spire, constructed on the site of a one-storey structure by the architects Yu. Shchuko and E. Stolyarov) and "Mechanization" (with a parabolic glass cupola,

348. Main entrance to the All-Russia Exhibition Centre (the former Exhibition of National Economic Achievements – VDNKh)

349. All-Russia Exhibition Centre.
The Worker and the Collective-Farm Woman. *1937. Sculptor V. Mukhina*

350

350. All-Russia Exhibition Centre.
Central alley with the Stone Flower *fountain*

→

351, 352. All-Russia Exhibition Centre.
Friendship of the Peoples *fountain. 1953. Architect
K. Topuridze and sculptor D. Konstantinovsky*

diameter 40 m; architects V. Andreyev and
I. Taranov, since 1966 its part with a
glass entrance arch houses the "Space"
exhibition). Located in the same axis are
the pompous red-granite *Friendship of the
Peoples* fountain, the *Stone Flower* fountain tiled with smalt (coloured glass) and
the *Ear of Wheat* fountain, 16 m high, on
Upper Pond.

The exhibition structures done in various historical styles and used to represent
different republics and regions of the
USSR were decorated by Alexander Deine-
ka, Boris Ioganson, Evgueny Lanceray,
Mikhail Manizer, Sergey Merkurov, Martiros
Saryan and many others.

Moscow Metro

Moscow's metro stations called the "underground palaces" are another attraction of the city. It is not an exaggeration as their interiors demonstrate almost royal splendour. Used in their decoration are more than twenty varieties of marble as well as labradorite, granite, porphyry, rhodonite, onyx and other natural stones. The first metro line began to operate in Moscow on May 15, 1935. The Moscow underground was designed and built by eminent Soviet architects who aimed not

353

354

353. *Underground vestibule of the metro station* Novoslobodskaya. *Stained-glass window. Painter P. Korin*

354. *Underground vestibule of the metro station* Mayakovskaya. *1938. Architect A. Dushkin*

355. *Underground vestibule of the metro station* Arbatskaya. *1953. Architects L. Polyakov and V. Pilevin*

356. *Underground vestibule of the metro station* Komsomolskaya-Koltsevaya. *1952. Architects A. Shchusev, V. Kakorin and A. Zabolotskaya*

357. *Underground vestibule of the metro station* Ploshchad Revolutsii. *1938. Architect A. Dushkin*

355

356

357

only at utility and comfort but gave every station a unique look. The metro station *Mayakovskaya* is considered one of the most beautiful. In 1937 it was awarded the Grand Prix at the International Exhibition in Paris as the first deep underground station supported with columns. The metro stations *Mayakovskaya*, *Kropotkinskaya*, *Prospect Mira* and *Kievskaya-Koltsevaya* are fine examples of architecture from the 1930s to 1950s. Some of them are protected by the state as national property.

361

358. Underground vestibule of the metro station Kievskaya-Koltsevaya. 1954. Architects E. Katonin, V. Skugarev and G. Golubev

359. Underground vestibule of the metro station Taganskaya-Koltsevaya. 1950. Architects K. Ryzhov and A. Medvedev

360. Underground vestibule of the metro station Sokol. 1938. Architects K. Yakovlev, V. Polikarpova and V. Andreyev

361. Underground vestibule of the metro station Aviamotornaya. 1979. Architects A. Strelkov, V. Klokov, N. Demchinsky and Yu. Kolesnikov

362. Underground vestibule of the metro station Park Pobedy. 2003. Architects M. Bubnov and V. Nikolayeva

363. Underground vestibule of the metro station Ulitsa Podbelskogo. 1990. Architects N. Alyoshin and N. Samoylov
→

364. Underground vestibule of the metro station Novoslobodskaya. 1952. Architects A. Dushkin and A. Strelkov

365

366

365. Northern River Port at Khimki. 1937.
Architects A. Rukhlyadev and V. Krinsky,
sculptor I. Yefimov

366. Detail of the facade decor of the Northern
River Port

367. Sculpture symbolizing the Canal of Moscow
at the entrance to the Northern River Port

→

368. Leningrad (former Nicholas)
Railway Station in Komsomolskaya Square.
1849. Architect K. Thon

River and Railway Stations

The Northern River Port is one of major Moscow's sights, noteworthy for its architecture. It looks like a huge steamer. An open gallery supported by 150 four-edged columns of white stone runs along the perimeter on its ground floor. The tower with its high spire, in the centre, resembles a navigating bridge. A wide granite staircase descends from the central portal to the main landing stage. Comfortable liners start from here on long voyages to Astrakhan, Rostov-on-Don and St Petersburg.

Moscow is a significant railway junction. Railways link it with big cities and small settlements of this great country as well as main European cities.

There are nine railway stations in Moscow, three of which (Leningrad, Kazan and Yaroslavl Railway Stations) are to be found in one square – Komsomolskaya, called by the citizens "the square of three stations."

The present-day Leningrad (former Nicholas) Railway Station is a replica of the Moscow Station built in St Petersburg. Trains leave it for St Petersburg, Petrozavodsk and Murmansk. Comfortable express trains (*Krasnaya Strela, Aurora, Russkaya Troika* and others) run between Moscow and St Petersburg.

→
369. Panoramic view of Komsomolskaya Square

→
370. View of the Kiev Railway Station from the Bogdan Khmelnitsky Bridge

→
371. Belarus (Belorussky) Railway Station. 1870. Reconstructed in 1909

372. Kiev Railway Station. 1912–17. Architect I. Rerberg

→
373. Platform of the Kazan Railway Station

→
374. Riga (Rizhsky) Railway Station. 1899–1902. Architect Yu. Diedericks

368

369

371

372

373

374

Modern Moscow

The section of Kalinin Prospect between Arbat Square and Sadovoye (Garden) Ring is another sight of present-day Moscow. The project worked out by a team of architects was awarded the Grand Prix by the Paris Centre of Architectural Research in 1966 for the renewal of architectural forms and achievements in working out long-term construction projects. The super

←
375. Kosmodamianskaya Embankment. Krasnye Kholmy business centre. Moscow International House of Music in the centre

376. Panoramic view of Moscow at night

377. View of the Bagration Bridge

378. Monument to Peter I. 1997. Sculptor Z. Tsereteli

modern style of this thoroughfare is made up by the geometrical regularity of its lines and the obvious repetitions and sharp contrasts of the forms. The verticals of the twenty-six-storey tower-shaped blocks rhythmically alternate with the lower, somewhat flattened, rectangular buildings that house cafes, bars, restaurants (including the *Tropicana* and *Metelitsa*) and shops (including the *Novoarbatsky*, a largest supermarket in the capital).

The light-coloured twenty-storey building that rises above the Krasnopresnenskaya Embankment is known as the White House, as it is the seat of Russia's government. Its design is rather peculiar. The building consists of two parts. Above the lower seven-storey part with sidewings there rises the narrower and taller part crowned by a small tower with a clock and the Russian Federation flag.

379

380

381

382

A broad staircase leads up to the entrance, in front of which there is a wide square. Before designing the edifice the author headed a group of architects who created the *Russia* hotel, the largest in Moscow.

379. Arbat Street. Pedestrian zone

380. Christmas and New Year illumination

381. Office of the Russian Federation Government on the Krasnopresnenskaya Embankment. 1981. Architect D. Chechulin

382. New Arbat. 1963–68. Architects M. Posokhin, A. Mndoyants, G. Makarevich, B. Tkhor, Sh. Ayrapetov, I. Pokrovsky, Yu. Popov and A. Zaytsev

383. Moscow cafe

383

384. Ostankino TV tower. 1960–67.
Engineer N. Nikitin, architects L. Batalova
and D. Burdina

385. Cosmos *hotel. 1976–79. Architects T. Zaikin,
V. Steiscal, Au. Cacoub, P. Jougleaux and S. Epstein.
Built by the "Seffrit" firm (France)*

386, 387. President *and* Renaissance
(Olympic Penta Hotel) *hotels, most fashionable
in Moscow*
→
388. *Memorial dedicated to the Victory in the Great
Patriotic War (WWII) of 1941–45 on Poklonnaya Hill.*
Music of Glory *fountain*

386

387

389

390

Moscow is a major tourist and business centre. Many comfortable hotels coming up to the highest standards have recently been erected here. The *Cosmos* (*Space*) hotel which can accommodate 3,600 people ranks among the hotels of the first international class. Located opposite the *VDNKh* metro station, in Mira (Peace) Prospect, the building was designed by Russian and French architects and engineers and

389. Grand fountain in the Equestrian Sports Centre. 1980. Sculptor Z. Tsereteli

390. Children are Victims of Adults' Sins. 2001. Sculptor M. Shemyakin

391. Victory Memorial dedicated to Russia's victory in the Great Patriotic War of 1941–45 on Poklonnaya Hill. 1983–95. Architects A. Polyansky, V. Budayev and L. Vavakin, sculptor Z. Tsereteli

constructed by a French firm. The upper part of this very tall structure comprising twenty-seven storeys has the shape of a semi-cylinder, or an arc. It forms a sort of mighty axis oriented towards the complex of the former Exhibition of Economic Achievements. Its facades are very impressive: their smoky goldish colour is created by the combination of the anodized aluminium of the walls and the dark-coloured glass of the windows. The buliding demonstrates a high quality of both construction and decoration work. The hotel has a well-equipped conference hall, a transformable banqueting hall, restaurants, cafes, bars, buffets, a swimming pool with a "beach" terrace, saunas and a bowling alley.

After the reconstruction the *Balchug* hotel has turned into a hotel of high European standard. The range of services provided and comfortableness put it among the most famous hotels of the world. The *Renaissance* (former *Olimpic*) and *President* (former *Oktyabrskaya*) are also de luxe hotels.

The Victory Memorial was opened in commemoration of the 50th anniversary of the victory in World War II (known in Russia as the Great Patriotic War). The memorial complex includes a museum (its displays are dedicated to the events of 1941–45), Conquerors' Square adorned with the allegorical figure of the goddess of Victory, "Years of War" alley and the Orthodox Church of St George decorated with huge bronze basreliefs. There is also a synagogue and a mosque.

Modern Moscow keeps on rapidly building dwelling houses and public structures, both in its centre and suburbs. New problems arise that had to be solved due to the very heavy traffic. One of the main projects is the construction of the third city "ring" (circular road). Moscow has been recently adorned with many new and restored old Christian Orthodox churches, most noteworthy of which are the churches of the Kazan Icon

392. Tverskaya Street

393

393. Dome of the Space Pavilion in the All-Russia Exhibition Centre

394, 395. Bagration Bridge. 2000. Architect Yu. Platonov

395

→
*396. Bogdan Khmelnitsky Bridge.
2002. Architect Yu. Platonov*

of the Mother of God (1991–93, architect O. Zhurin) in Red
Square, the Icon of the Mother of God "Assuage My Sorrow"
at Maryino, St Tychon at Liublino and the Chapel of the Nativity of the Mother of God in Stoleshnikov Lane.

New architectural forms have enriched the Moscow scenery. Many foot-bridges have been recently constructed. The capital's leading architects are Yu. Grigoryev, M. Leonov, A. Skokan, A. Trofimov, M. Posokhin, P. Andreyev, S. Tkachenko and others, they design both houses and public buildings.

397. Moscow-City
International business
centre. Federation office
complex

398. Sergey Obraztsov's
Central Puppet Theatre.
Detail of the facade

399. Complex of the
Moscow Government
buildings. 1963–70.
Architects M. Posokhin
and A. Mndoyants

400. Raushskaya
Embankment.
View of the Balchug-
Kempinski hotel
and Centrobank building

401. Ostankino TV tower

402. Novy (New) Arbat at night

403. Kamergersky Lane

404. Trubnaya Square
→
405. Panoramic view
of the Moscow River

402

403

404

Trinity–St Sergius Monastery

The famous Trinity–St Sergius Monastery where ascetic life has not ceased up to now is situated in 56 km from Moscow on the road to Yaroslavl. It was founded by St Sergius (1314–1392) who had come to live in the then deserted and desolate place on the bank of the Kochura River from the nearby town of Radonezh in 1335. He and his brother constructed here a wooden Church of the Holy Trinity. The monastery was formed in the 1340s. St Sergius was greatly revered by Russian people for his spiritual gifts and when Prince Dmitry Donskoy went to fight with the Tartars, he came to ask for his blessing.

The monastery's magnificent ensemble was built from the 15th to 19th centuries. The oldest extant structure is the white-stone Cathedral of the Holy Trinity erected

406, 408. Trinity–St Sergius Monastery. Founded in 1337

*407. Main entrance to the monastery.
So-called "Red Gate." 16th – 19th centuries*

408

409. Panoramic view
of the Trinity–St Sergius
Monastery

410

411   412

by abbot Nicon in 1422–23. The money for the construction was donated by Moscow Prince Vasily I and Zvenigorod Prince Yury Dmitrievich. This rare example of early Moscow architecture is similar in style to the Dormition Cathedral in Zvenigorod (1399). Annexed to the cathedral on the south is the wing of St Nicon built over the grave of abbot Nicon in 1548 (reconstructed in 1623).

The Cathedral of the Holy Trinity was erected to commemorate St Sergius' immense service to the state. Here at St Sergius' shrine Moscow princes kissed the cross swearing to keep their promises and treaties and prayed before going to wars and on coming back from them.

Inside the Trinity Cathedral was painted in 1425–27 by the famous icon-painters Andrey Rublev, Daniil Chorny and their assistants. Unfortunately, in 1635 their

410. Pyatnitskaya Tower. 1640

411. Church of Sts Zosimas and Sabbatius of Solovki, with a hipped roof, in the monastery hospital. 1635–37

412. Churches of the Entry into the Temple (1547) and St Parasceva (17th century)

413. Krasnogorskaya Chapel. 1770

414. Bell tower. 1740–70. Architects I. Michurin and D. Ukhtomsky

415

416

417

frescoes were replaced with new ones which
have been also repainted not once. Yet the
unique iconostasis, many icons for which
were executed by Andrey Rublev (one of
them was the famous *Holy Trinity*, now
in the State Tretyakov Gallery) has survived.

The silver shrine of St Sergius commissioned by Ivan the Terrible in 1585 graces
the cathedral. It is to be found near
the south wall in front of the iconostasis.
The canopy was set up over it in 1737.
It is one of the main places of pilgrimage
for Orthodox Christians. In the iconostasis

417. Icon: Exaltation of the Cross *(late 16th
century) from the village of Vozdvizhenskoye*

*415. Cathedral of the Dormition. Iconostasis.
Early 18th century*

*418. Trinity–St Sergius Monastery.
Cathedral of the Dormition. 1559–85.
Chapel on the well. Late 17th century*

*416. Icon of St Sergius of Radonezh.
Second half of the 15th century*

419. In the Trinity–St Sergius Monastery

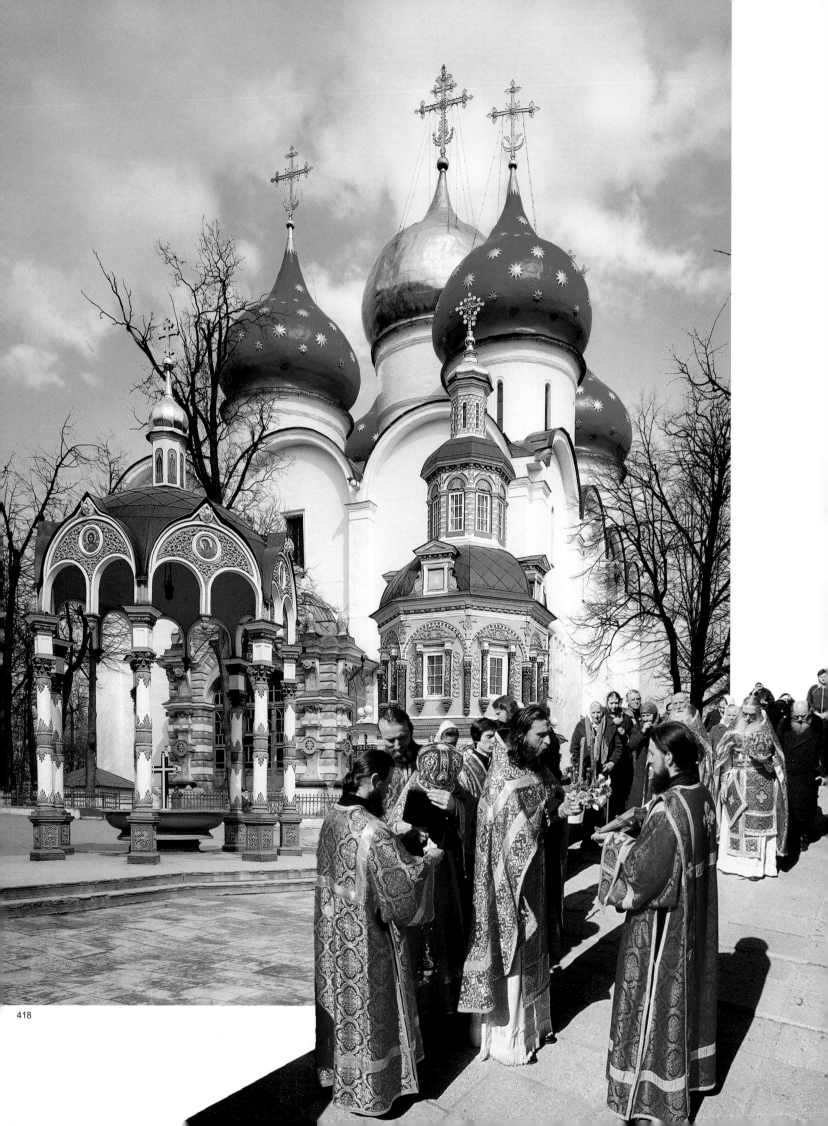

above the shrine there used to be the icon of St Nicholas dating from the first third of the 14th century. It is supposed to have been the family icon of St Sergius' parents and now is kept in the monastery museum.

Opposite the Trinity Cathedral there stands the Church of the Holy Spirit, or the Church of the Descent of the Holy Spirit on the Apostles, built in 1476–77 by Pskov masters. The structure is unusual for 15th-century Moscow architecture as it has bell chimes installed in its drum and supported by six heavy pillars.

The most important building in the ensemble is the Cathedral of the Dormition (1559–85) modelled, like many churches from the epoch of Ivan the Terrible, on the Kremlin cathedral of the same name. Its spacious interior is remarkable for the paintings done in 1684 and carved iconostasis in the so-called "Naryshkin" Baroque style. A small stone structure with a hipped roof by its north-west corner

420, 422. In the museum rooms

421. Vestry. Gospel. 1754. Moscow

423. Icon of St Nicholas, the Old Testament Trinity and selected saints. 1592

424. Vestry. Mitre. 1626

422

423

424

425

houses the tombs of Boris Godunov and his
family.

The most festive-looking buildings in the
ensemble are the Refectory Church with its
side-altar dedicated to St Sergius (1686–92)
and the chapel on the well near the Dormition Cathedral (late 17th century), they
demonstrate a refined polychrome decor,
characteristic of the Moscow Baroque style.
A fine sample of structures with hipped
roofs is the Church of Sts Zosimas and Sabbatius of Solovki in the hospital (1635–37).
Built in the 17th century were also the
gateway Church of the Nativity of St John
the Baptist (1693–99, the money was

425. Cathedral of the Holy Trinity.
View of the iconostasis and St Sergius' shrine

426. Cathedral of the Holy Trinity. 1422–23

427. Frame of the icon of the Holy Trinity
by Andrey Rublev. 1600

427

given by G. Stroganov), houses of monks' cells and the royal palace (for members of the royal family on pilgrimage) with tiled stoves (mid-18th century).

The 18th-century buildings include the Church of St Micah (1734, 1746) with an intricate "Dutch" roof and the rotunda-shaped Church of the Smolensk Icon of the Mother of God (1746–48) constructed with the donation of Count A. Razumovsky.

The dominant feature of the ensemble and its tallest structure is the five-tier bell tower. Begun in 1740 by Ivan Michurin, it was completed only in 1770 after the design of D. Ukhtomsky.

One of the leading exponents of the Enlightenment in Russia, Metropolitan Platon initiated redecoration of the metropolitan residence (1778) and installation of the tetrahedral obelisk "glorifying the monastery" (1792).

The monastery is enclosed with a fortified wall decorated by four octahedral (in the corners) and seven tetrahedral towers (round the perimeter), built in the 1540s. In the 17th century their height was increased twice. The wall consists of three defence tiers. The lower one contains deeply set casemates and embrasures, the middle tier is a vaulted gallery with loopholes and the upper one is a gallery with battlements.

Outside the monastery the brotherhood owns the churches of the Entry into the Temple (1547) and St Parasceva (late 17th century), which had been the property of the Podolny St Parasceva Monastery until 1660, as well as the Krasnogorskaya Chapel (1770) and many other buildings.

Since 1814 the Moscow Theological Academy has been located on the territory of the monastery. Founded in 1685, it is the oldest higher educational institution in Russia.

428. Trinity–St Sergius Monastery. Refectory Church. Detail of the facade

429. Trinity–St Sergius Monastery. Refectory Church. Interior

430. Trinity–St Sergius Monastery. Refectory with the Church of St Sergius of Radonezh. 1686–92

429

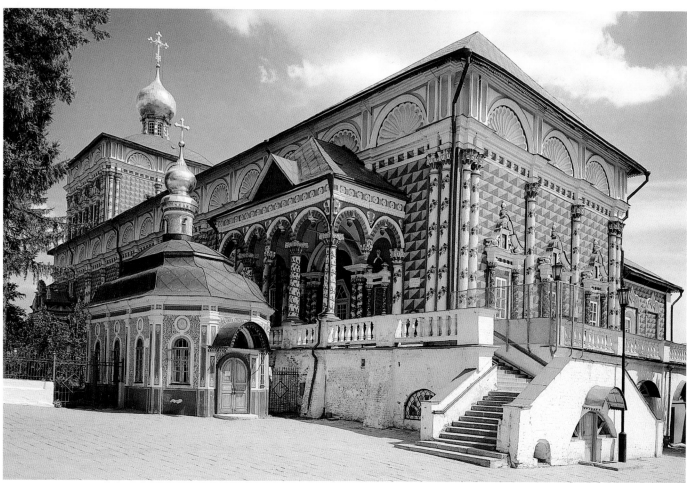

430

431

In 1920 the museum-preserve of art and history was opened here. Its holdings comprise priceless early Russian icons and other works of religious art. Among them are one of the earliest icons of St Sergius (15th century) and two-tier icon of the Exaltation of the Cross (second half of the 16th century) coming from the village of Vozdvizhenskoye situated on the road to Moscow.

431. View of the Dormition Cathedral from the Refectory window

432. Gateway Church of St John the Baptist. 1693–99

433

433. Gateway Church of St John the Baptist.
Interior

Contents

Москва

Альбом на английском языке

Издательство «П-2», Санкт-Петербург

Торговый дом «Медный всадник»
www.mvsadnik.ru. Тел./факс (812) 320-91-35

Изготовитель ООО «Новатор»
Россия, 197101, Санкт-Петербург, ул. Мира, д. 3. Тел./факс (812) 495-61-46

Бумага мелованная, печать офсетная